T0105351

MOON ENERGY

Helios Press books may be purchased in bulk at special discounts for sales
promotion, corporate gifts, fund-raising, or educational purposes. Special
editions can also be created to specifications. For details, contact the Special
Sales Department, Skyhorse Publishing, 307 West 36th Street, 11th Floor, New
York, NY 10018 or info@skyhorsepublishing.com.

Helios® and Helios Press® are registered trademarks of Skyhorse Publishing,
Inc.®, a Delaware corporation.

Visit our website at www.skyhorsepublishing.com.

10 9 8 7 6 5 4

Library of Congress Cataloging-in-Publication Data is available on file.

Cover design by Daniel Brount
Cover illustration by Vic Oh
Direction : Jean-Lous Hocq
Editorial direction : Suyapa Hammje
Edition : Lama Younès-Corm
Manufacturing : Céline Premel-Cabig
Engraving : Les Caméléons
Graphic creation and realization : Guylaine Moi

Print ISBN: 978-1-5107-5403-4
Ebook ISBN: 978-1-5107-5404-1

Printed in China

STÉPHANIE LAFRANQUE

VIC OH

MOON
ENERGY

A PRACTICAL GUIDE TO USING LUNAR CYCLES
TO UNLEASH YOUR INNER GODDESS

TRANSLATED BY GRACE MCQUILLAN

Helios
press

CONTENTS

FOREWORD

As a child I was timid and polite. I didn't roll around in the dirt but I was a little animal nonetheless and all of my senses were highly attuned. I could smell perfumes and other odors from miles away, I could hear everything around me, I loved the taste of new things and the feel of water, flowers, and herbs under my fingers. I spent a lot of time with my grandmother and she would tell me all about plants and pagan festivals as if it were the most natural thing in the world. Then one day she passed down her gift to me: the art of dreaming. I learned that the Moon was my companion. With all six of my senses now awakened, I felt complete. But time passed, I grew up, and I forgot. I shrugged off my fur to put on clothing. Twelve years ago, I had my first child, a daughter. It was then, curled up in the midst of becoming a mother, that I started hearing things clearly again, seeing beyond the visible world, noticing the smells that surrounded me, feeling every cell wriggle as I ate, and sensing people's energies whenever I touched their bodies. I had remembered my original skin, so I took a step in its direction and stopped using chemical contraception so I could realign with my natural cycles. One night, long after she had passed away, my grandmother came to me in a dream to give me a message: answer the call of the Moon. I understood what she was offering me. She was bringing me back my fur.

Now it's my turn, and I am inviting every woman trying to connect with her original nature to follow me through this book. The Moon is our age-old companion and guides us back to ourselves. The way our societies insist upon burying the memory of this lunar connection says something about the level of fear that female power can elicit. And yet, from the beginning of time, the tempo of this celestial body has guided our steps with her four phases and two movements. These moments in the lunar cycle are universal and cosmic transitions that mirror every part of life: birth, growth, decline, death, and ascending or descending energy.

I believe that if we connect ourselves to this cycle, we will discover that we also carry it inside of us. In turn we will live a more natural life and (re) become who we really are. We will learn to better understand ourselves and listen to ourselves more carefully so that we can reclaim our individual power. This ancient knowledge and a practice of attentive listening to our inner selves will guide us on the path to discovering the goddess within.

In the midst of this chaotic world, something powerful is calling us. Our place as women is being redefined and an equilibrium is starting to establish itself in the bond between humans and nature. Respecting our essence means respecting our Earth and feeling at home in our place in the universe. Our time has come: like the priestesses in the ancient temples, let's become guardians of the Moon, Moon goddesses. Let's learn to decipher her energies, read her phases, feel her passing through the constellations, use the lunar archetypes, rediscover the ancestral wisdom of magic plants, and usher ritual into our lives. During the New Moon and Full Moon— the two great energetic portals of the month— let's draw upon the natural forces at work to live out our own cyclicity. Like the ocean tides, we all have our own inner movements. Revealing them makes us aware of the impermanence of all things and allows us to feel that we belong to a system greater than ourselves.

Let's reclaim this wild woman knowledge; let's listen to the stirrings of our earth-belly. Let's become what, deep down, we always have been: independent, free, and creative.

I'd like to mention here two of the women who have shown me this path. The first is psychoanalyst Clarissa Pinkola Estès. In her book *Women Who Run with The Wolves*, Estès uses the word *wild* in its original sense, which means to live a natural life, binding together what is intimate and universal. She encourages us to follow our instincts because it guides our understanding of the interior and exterior worlds. The second woman is an American ecofeminist, Starhawk, who calls women to reconnect with their essence, their intuition, and to listen to their inner movements and understand how to use this process each day to reactivate "the power-from-within." A lunar woman is a "wild woman" who cares for her inner ecology just as she cares for the ecology of the planet. In a society where everything moves quickly, where everything is consumable, let's return to wisdom and authenticity. Let's choose instead this life of cycles, in all of its richness, intimacy, and respect. Let's watch over our sisters and the world and free ourselves from all domination. Let us be sovereign over our realm, guardians of our well-being—and of the Moon.

ONCE UPON A TIME, THERE WAS THE MOON . . .

The Moon, because of her cyclical nature, is changing every night. Just like us, she is always present but never exactly the same, and she seems to understand our existence as human beings lost in the midst of the cosmos. We feel less alone because of her sweet presence. I invite each one of you to weave your own lunar story every month and embrace your desire to connect with this ancient wisdom, because the Moon was a companion to our societies long before the written word ever mentioned her. Every culture instinctively created a language to converse with her. Whether humans were deep in caves, inside the ancient temples, or in the heart of the forests of the pre-Christian era, this bond has never been broken. She still shines above our heads today, but our Western societies have forgotten that she is our guide. And so, in the purity of the night, she watches over us and waits for us to make contact with her once again.

○ PRIMITIVE SOCIETIES

Imagine yourself barefoot. The cries of nocturnal animals fill the glacial silence of the night. You lift your face to the sky. The Moon is full; your only source of light. You have been waiting for this moment. This is perhaps what the first women found themselves doing each month, coming out of their caves to admire the twinkling celestial body. They would have been the first to understand the obvious synchronicity of our cycles: the Moon's cycle is 29 days long and begins at each New Moon, and a woman's menstrual cycle usually lasts between 28 and 30 days. This made the Moon our first reference point for measuring the passage of time. Her four movements correspond to the stages of all life, and this connection is depicted with great precision on Neolithic pottery. Even earlier, during the Paleolithic period, Europeans used bones to create the first lunar calendars: the New Moon served as the starting point for each cycle and notches were carved into the bone to mark each phase. Menstrual cycles and pregnancies are also recorded on these artifacts.

This is perhaps the first acknowledgement that woman, like the Moon, dies and is reborn every month. During this same period, from 25,000 to 3,000 BC, the "Great Goddess," or "Mother Goddess," was worshipped by many people throughout Europe. She is depicted in a variety of forms, from a bird goddess painted in the Pech Merle grotto in France in 15,000 BC to chevrons, Ms, and Vs on handmade vases and fertility statues linking water to women and the Moon. The Great Goddess also appears in famous bas-relief carvings, like the Venus of Laussel carved into a block of limestone in Dordogne, and sculptures including the Venus of Lespugue in Haute-Garonne, the Venus of Willendorf in Austria, and the Venus of Brassempouy in the Landes region of France. All of them depict curvaceous women, snake women, or bird goddesses adorned with elements associated with the lunar cycle: crescents, circles, horns with notches marking thirteen moons, and drawings of the yoni (the female genital organ). These symbols of life were also created to celebrate fertility, magic, and death.

○ COSMOGONIES

Moon worship was widespread in many cultures during the pre-Christian era, including Ancient Greece, Rome, and Mesopotamia. Depictions of the celestial body as a deity were frequent, and she appears in creation myths with both masculine and feminine traits. She incarnates the potent first creative force that gave birth to the Sun and Universe.

With the advent of writing in 3,000 BC, and as the patriarchy began to supplant the matriarchy, the Sun became the more venerated heavenly body. In spite of this radical change, the Moon maintained her bond with inner feminine power and preserved her spiritual influence.

In ancestral myths from the Inuits, Egyptians, Sumerians, Aztecs, and Celts, the Sun and Moon are revered and often presented as a couple, or in a trio with the Earth. The Moon is usually punished for having caused some offense, forcing her to shine less brightly than her companion the Sun. Out of shame and a need to hide herself, she is only able to appear at night. It is interesting to note that a celestial body linked to a woman and her cycles was only blamed for her faults and forced to bear the weight of repentance once patriarchal cultures appeared. In Sumerian cosmogony, which is also one of the most ancient, the Earth and Sky are one until Enlil, the wind god, splits them apart and they are separated into two different planes: the Sky, above, symbolizing masculinity, and the Earth, below, symbolizing femininity. Enlil's lover gives birth to a moon god named Sin (or Nanna) who creates light by bringing forth the Sun and Venus. He later becomes one of the major gods because of his generosity toward mankind and symbolizes protection, fertility, and above all, light in the midst of darkness.

In later years, a number of moon goddesses including Hecate, Selene, Artemis, and Ishtar also made their appearance. The priestesses who worshipped these goddesses were "virgins," meaning they were liberated from all matrimonial engagement, and performed naked rituals to honor the Moon using fire and water.

○ SHAMANS

One group of practices that intimately connects human beings to the cosmos, natural cycles, and, therefore, to the Moon has existed since the dawn of time: shamanism. Shamanism bears the hallmarks of the cultures it was born into and integrates the stories and myths of these peoples into its craft and spiritual rites. Its strength lies in its ability to bind worlds together: the physical one in which we live, and the subtle universes that surround us. Every civilization has encountered shamanism at one time or another and some have found it to be fertile ground for their societal equilibrium while others have replaced it with more dogmatic religious practices. In any case, from the boreal forests of Siberia where shamanism began to the remote lands of Africa and the Americas, the shaman figure is viewed as a point of access to the invisible world and a channel between the telluric and cosmic forces who heals souls and bodies through ecstatic journeys and trances. In the Western world, this spiritual relationship with nature can be seen in the druids and druidesses who played an important role in Celtic civilizations.

Shamanism has taken on many forms since the Archaic period, but there are some common elements—like the "World Tree" or "Cosmic Mountain" connecting the world below to the world above—that remain intact. This cross-cultural symbol of the *axis mundi*, or world axis, borrows its two energetic movements, growth and decline (the Full Moon and Black Moon), from the Moon's cycle, and shamanic practices use the position of stars and planets like the Big Dipper and the Moon. Lunar motifs are also found in descriptions of the World Tree, particularly in Siberia where, like the Moon, this tree embodies fertility, initiation, and the cycle of life and death. In Assyria, a tree trunk crowned with a crescent is a motif commonly used in depictions of the Moon god, and the tree is a recurring image in lunar worship practices and Moon goddess allegories.

The Moon's roundness is also powerfully present in the Native American medicine wheel, which has its roots in shamanic practices and overlaps with the lunar cycle. Round like the Full Moon and divided into several phases, the medicine wheel incorporates the four cardinal directions: north for the New Moon, south for the Full Moon, west for the last quarter, and east for the first quarter. It also depicts the four elements, the four ages of life, the four seasons, and infinite rebirth, all of which are themes associated with the lunar cycle.

The drum, which beats like a heart and generates a magical force capable of transporting us to explore limitless planes of being, is the instrument of shamanic journeys and rituals. It is made of wood to symbolize the World Tree and its stretched animal hide is reminiscent of the silver celestial body in its whiteness and shape. In certain communities like the Sámi people of Scandinavia, the drum is also decorated with paintings of the Moon or Sun.

Today shamanism is widespread throughout the Western world and many people, especially women, use it to reconnect to their cyclicity and their bond with nature. According to American lecturer and shaman Vicki Noble, each month when a woman bleeds, a "shamanic healing" that cleans away the past is taking place. This discharge is seen as a necessary death, a molting that only females and lunar cycles are capable of. We sense a kind of hidden dimension boiling in our blood, and these "moons" or menstruations awaken a sacred vibration in us. This is why shamanic healing rituals are often performed during the great lunar phases of the New Moon and Full Moon. If this call makes something vibrate within you, know how to listen to it. Performing ceremonies at these times can be a good first step down this path and a way to discover your ability to connect with the Universe in a concrete way.

○ WITCHES

This word is often said in a whisper, already carrying the ritual in itself. "Witch" was, is, and will be what remains of the wild in our humanity. It is a wildness that is in no way demonic or barbaric, but is instead akin to liberty, emancipation, and an ability to be self-sufficient and live in osmosis with the laws of nature.

From the pictures in our children's books, where they are always depicted as cruel and ugly women, to the contemporary image of the unapologetic feminist, witches have always titillated the collective imagination. When we talk about them, we often imagine women roaming the land in the middle of the night or flying on broomsticks to perform strange ceremonies together. In their coven (or clan) witches unite for meetings called esbats every Full Moon and Sabbat ceremonies at certain times during the lunar year. Sabbats have their roots in Dionysian celebrations that were held to honor the horned god who would later become synonymous with the devil in the Middle Ages. Witchcraft's connection to lunar cycles has made the Moon as much a symbol of the witch as the cauldron, magic plants, or the black cat.

We cannot mention this folkloric representation of the witch without also discussing witch hunts and the blood that was spilled on our Western lands for centuries. These murders were born out of a hatred for women, an ancestral hatred that stems from Genesis and Eve, the bearer of original sin, who makes all women intrinsically sinful beings. Contrary to popular belief, witch persecution was not at its worst in the Middle Ages; this came later and took on terrifying dimensions between the late fifteenth and early eighteenth centuries. Society needed time before it was ready to commit such terrible acts and embrace such complete anti-feminism in response to the desires of the ruling classes: to divide the poor at a time when there were rumblings of revolt and to take power away from women, who were considered inferior beings. Those accused of witchcraft were peasants, healers, and usually elderly, but most importantly they were women who lived unsupervised by men. To society, their independence represented a danger that had to be eradicated at all costs. Witch, "saga," *sage femme* (wise woman): everything was already there in the words themselves. People turned to them because of their herbal knowledge and because they were often the only people, especially in the countryside, who could treat diseases. The university system, by institutionalizing the practice of medicine, ripped it out of the hands of these female experts to seal it away under masculine authority. Once this appropriation was complete, all that was left to do was make them disappear, muffle their voices, and burn their bodies. Despite this terrible repression, witches' powerful oral culture has been passed down through the centuries. A variety of rituals that worship the Sun god and Moon goddess allow this pagan knowledge to continue circulating, and the Moon, her cycle, and her phases remain essential points of reference marking the completion of pagan ceremonies and energetic work.

The new spirituality that is rising around the witch figure today combines reliance on the elements, reappropriation of female power, and political awareness. A stream called Wicca has been developing steadily in Anglo-Saxon countries since the early twentieth century. There are several Wiccan branches, but all of them rely on the pagan traditions and advocate a return to the forces of nature, connection to the elements, and freedom to practice. In this reappropriation of her individual power, woman is restoring the image of the witch. She is choosing to construct herself not in opposition to the masculine, but in equilibrium between the two polarities that exist in all beings and things.

If we recognize that our commitment to ourselves and our well-being is also a pledge of allegiance to the Earth that carries us, then now more than ever the witch holds a critical role in a world that is being hit full force by ecological catastrophe. With her connection to and her understanding of the cycles of nature, she can probe its depths to forge a bond between Mother Earth and the Moon. She is a vehicle for a relationship with the elemental world that is founded on respect and deep exchange and she embodies the notion of inner ecology.

WOMAN: A LUNAR BEING

Every woman speaks the lunar language, even if we have forgotten our knowledge of its wisdom. By working with these cycles, we become aware of the impermanence of our lives. We too evolve according to a cyclical dynamic, and our essence, that of our wild woman, desires to be in motion. When we choose to take this initiatory path, we begin to match the rhythm of seasonal energies. We become star, wild grass, and river, and are no longer familiar with immobility or immutability because we enter into the great cosmic movement. This awakening, which begins with the sap rising during the spring equinox, will take on different shades of color throughout the year. Our coats will change, darken, become covered in copper and gold, and we will return to our innerness and experience a deep cleansing as we free ourselves from residual energies. We will learn to listen to our own rhythm, advancing at our own speed. Doesn't this sound wonderful already? Learn to listen to your needs, follow your intuition, and become your own energy channel. By taking care of yourself, you will know better how to take care of others.

○ OUR FEMININE CYCLE

We have a menstrual cycle that typically lasts 28 days and echoes the "synodic" lunar revolution lasting 29.5 days: the time to go from one New Moon to the next. Everything that is born will one day die. As women, we carry this cycle within us each month. It is part of how we function: menstruation, postmenstrual phase, ovulation, premenstrual phase, menstruation. When we do not take these changes into account, we deprive ourselves of a tool of self-knowledge, we give no consideration to our inner movements, and we do not understand our cyclical states. Use a lunar calendar to study the connection between your cycle and the phases of the Moon. Many of you will notice that you menstruate during the New or Full Moon. If this is not the case, begin connecting yourself to her more closely and you will see your cycle begin to harmonize with her phases in the same way that women living in community with each other often have their moons (menstrual cycles) at the same time.

In the Native American tradition, women who were menstruating would gather in moon lodges. These were spaces where they could meet to celebrate their menstruation and be relieved of daily tasks. The moon lodge was reserved especially for them and each woman played a role in this space considered sacred by the entire community. During this time of voluntary distancing they would connect directly with the Moon and their uteruses to develop their spirituality, intuition, and their capacities as dreamers in the Universe and among all forms of life: Mother Earth, plants, and animals. These women could freely live their innerness for an interval of four days, like the four seasons, the four directions, the four elements (Earth, Fire, Wind, Water), and the four Moon phases. At one time this distancing was considered purifying, benevolent, and rewarding. Now, however, we have forgotten the deep meaning of this rite and have transformed this inner journey of menstruation into a forced exile. Menstrual blood has become taboo today. We need to give it back the recognition it deserves so that an archaic fear of the mystery of creation—and a fear of the uterus as a place where life is formed—will no longer guide the collective unconscious.

It should also be noted that it is possible to connect with your cycle even if you are using contraception. It will simply take a little bit more time, more interaction, and more listening to the self, because while you are on the pill your cycle is sleeping and you are not ovulating. Don't become fixated on the periods of your bleeding, but instead on what you feel and how it correlates with the lunar phases. When you return to your feminine cycle, you reconnect yourself to the movements of life and enter into an apprenticeship to become that wild woman once again. You have a space to reclaim, a peaceful balance to find, and a healing to offer the world.

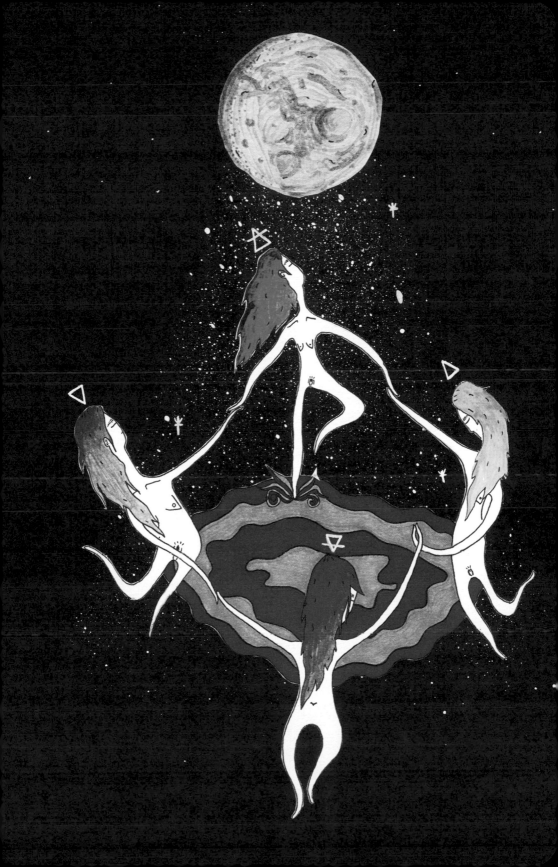

○ THE PHASES OF YOUR CYCLE

INTERIORITY

The New Moon corresponds with the period of menstruation. This is the night goddess phase when energies are more interior, more somber, and the correlations with nature are winter and the Earth element. Take care of your inner world during this time; leave your fields fallow, at rest, and welcome in the empty and obscure, honoring your earth to make it more fertile for the future. In this unique moment of alignment with your inner power, remember to slow down, rest, and embrace your heightened sensitivity and intuition in the form of dreams and visions.

POWER

During the first quarter, when the Moon is ascending, feminine energy is also increasing. This is the active phase of preovulation, the phase of the dawn goddess that mirrors the springtime and the Wind element. You are awakening to the revival taking place within you and you are filled with powerful energies. Pioneering, independent, and dynamic, you move with vigor toward your objectives. It is a time for decision-making and concrete actions.

RADIANCE

The Full Moon corresponds with the ovulation period, the powerful moment of femininity, maternity, and creation. This is the phase of the zenith goddess, summer, and the Fire element. It is a time of radiance, and you are at the height of your strength. Your inner energies are strong and stable enough to allow you to turn yourself toward the exterior. You are proactive and emit an overflowing vitality that offers attention, love, softness, and generosity to others in the midst of your own intense creative stirrings.

INSTINCT

In the last quarter, during the Moon's descending phase, you follow the path of your innerness and intuition. This is the premenstrual phase, the twilight goddess phase that is linked to autumn and the Water element. It is a return to your Earth, a time in which your instinct is your guide. Be especially mindful of your body and emotions as you initiate a descent into your own depths and pay special attention to imagination and creative inspiration.

I would also like to speak to women who are in menopause and no longer bleed. I have noticed what a painful journey this can be in our societies, where many women find it difficult to embrace and are not given sufficient support. I have heard words like "shame," "rejection," "disgust," and "death," which are intolerable descriptions of something that is in the nature of things. This verbal violence makes me realize just how little we are able to take care of ourselves; we don't know how to see the sacred within us because no one has shown us the path to do so.

The premenopausal and menopausal periods are disorienting for women. There is a kind of loss of identity. What does it mean to be a woman when we can no longer bear children? What kind of value is attributed to this passage in our lives? How do we talk about it? What words resonate in our ears? Quite often the feeling of a void will emerge, because the only things about this time that are discussed are the symptoms we try to get rid of as quickly as possible. Just as we still tell young women today to live their lives as if their menstrual cycle didn't exist, we often try to do the same with women going through menopause. I would like us to be aware of the new power that lives within us during this time because it is in this moment that our creative energies pass into another dimension of the body. Our personal cycle, our sexuality, and our desire now have all the space they need to fully blossom. In some cultures, including the Native American tradition, menopause is a time when we come closer to the Goddess and become wise. We have more freedom than before and a knowledge of the woman and the body that we now know how to listen to. We become messengers and guides for our sisters. Our power is more consistent. We fully embrace the lunar cycles to make them coincide with our inner rhythm. We are attentive to our bodies in accordance with another frequency. It is a new connection but the bond is still just as present.

For women who no longer have a uterus, you should know that the energetic trace will always remain. Even though many women have trouble feeling this part of their bodies, and even if this absence is painful, the same work can still be done. It is possible to find the path of this vibration in our center. Energetic techniques like reiki, shiatsu, and kundalini or yin yoga can serve us on this path to reappropriation.

○ CONNECTING WITH NATURE

Listening to the song of lunar energies connects you deeply with the Earth. Being in contact with nature can help facilitate this process. Even though not all of us are able to dive into the natural world on a daily basis, be careful not to weaken this bond, especially if you live in a city. Be aware that nature is everywhere around you. You can connect just as much to a tree near your house or a succulent growing in your home as you can to an entire forest. Accept that all of these beings have the same value and just as much to share with you, because anything that is living is also powerful.

Begin by observing what is vibrating around your home, in a park, on the beach, in the forest, and in other places that allow you to reanchor and regenerate, where you can lay down your body and the energies that surround it and fill yourself with the high vibrations that you find. If you live in a very urban area, relearn how to connect—how to feel, in other words—even if most of the time you feel cut off from this beneficial environment. To check the weather today we no longer open our windows, we just look at our smartphones. Resharpen your senses (those of the wild woman within you) and activate your lunar soul as you discover, through yourself and through your body, your ability to sense the world.

Take time to observe nature every day, to listen (birds singing, the sound of rain, a gust of wind) to feel (cold, heat), to smell (flowers, trees), touch (stones, bark, grass), and taste (snow, rain). Even if it's only five minutes a day, connect by placing one hand on a tree or watering your plants. Do what feels right for you, but make it a conscious choice. Inviting nature into your life will help you move in the direction of ancient knowledge and respect for the vegetal world and will open the way for communication with living things and your wild nature.

Connecting with the Moon involves a connection with both the Earth and Sky. You have deep roots that anchor you firmly and allow you to lift yourself up as high as you can go. You can become a bridge between the two.

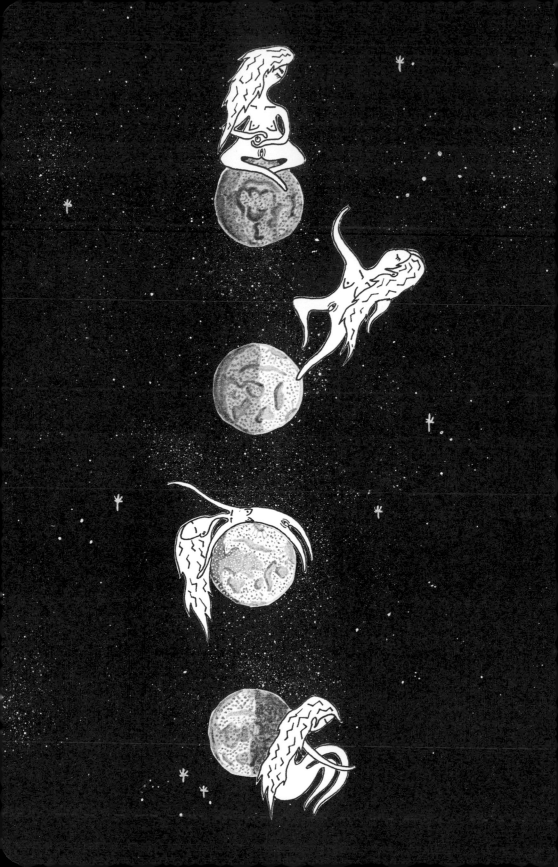

THE MOON REVEALED

To understand the Moon, we have to find out a little more about her: her cycles, the meaning behind her poetic names, her colors, and the energies that emerge from each of her phases. All of these things help us know her better; she is far away but she is also so close to us and is our ally. The cosmos is the theater where the Moon performs, and the sky is the stage on which she unveils her movements to us. I invite you, through the use of a calendar, to examine her positions so that you too can join in the great lunar dance.

○ NEW MOON: DAYS 1–7

This marks the beginning of the lunar cycle. The Moon no longer appears in the sky and instead we catch a glimpse of her hiding behind a dark circle. Her visible side is in shadow. This is the time when the night is blackest.

ENERGIES

This is the phase of naked dancing and the night goddess. It is conducive to meditations, divinations, and prophetic dreams. The energies act like a blank page and it is possible to go back to zero and reinvent yourself. Set your intentions, cleanse your energies, and purify your living spaces. This is the chance to let go of what no longer serves you. This moment of rebirth is ideal for creating new projects, writing them down, and preparing before putting them into action. From now on energy will only continue to increase until the Full Moon.

FIRST QUARTER: DAYS 8–14

You are in a period of growth. Beginning at the New Moon, the luminous surface of the Moon starts to increase, or "wax." You have entered the phase of the first crescent and the Moon appears perfectly split in two: half in darkness, half in the light. The bright side is now on the right: the trick to remembering this is to imagine a vertical line between the dark part and the light part so that it forms the letter "p" like "primary," meaning "first."

ENERGIES

This is the phase of beginnings, ascending energies, the dawn goddess, and the intense rhythms of tribal dances. You attract positive thoughts and open a period of prosperity that is conducive to "doing," putting new plans into action, and blossoming relationships. You open yourself to others and to the world and your desire to share and collaborate is very present. This is also a phase of intense creation and imagination. Use the energies at work to reinforce, develop, improve, enlarge, and fertilize a project. It is the ideal time to make your body an ally and to push your physical abilities and endurance further. The first quarter is by far the most conducive to putting your healing in place and setting intentions of abundance.

FULL MOON: DAYS 15–22

The Moon is in full bloom at the height of her brightness, power, and influence. She brings fertility to our projects and promotes spiritual connection. Her energies are very present and can be felt three days before and two or three days after. The Full Moon has a unique and forceful influence and she functions like a pump, eliminating old energies to fill us with new ones. If you are highly perceptive, you may experience discomfort around Full Moons. It is a good idea to learn how to anticipate and utilize these moments so you don't have to suffer from her strong influence during this time.

ENERGIES

During the Full Moon we honor spirits and energies: this is the phase of the zenith goddess and your power is at its peak. Undertake rituals of gratitude and connection and use the moonlight to consecrate the objects used in your spiritual practices by charging your stones, crystals, and divination tools beneath its rays. This is the phase of the star dance, an expression of our desire to honor the Moon through movement by using the energies of the moment.

This is also a significant period for dreams, and the nights are a fertile time. Like your body, your mind is experiencing "inner tides" that throw you off balance and cause interrupted sleep, agitation, and insomnia. Take advantage of this power to form a deep connection with your spirituality (one that is secular, like mine, or one that matches your personal beliefs).

LAST QUARTER: DAYS 23–29

The third day after the Full Moon, we enter into a phase of decreasing, or "waning." The bright surface of the celestial body begins to diminish in size. The Moon is once again split in two: half dark, half light. To spot the quarter, imagine once more a vertical line through the center and look for the "d" like "decreasing" that appears.

ENERGIES

You are now in a phase where energies are at their lowest: the phase of the twilight goddess and instinctive dance, a choreography that is guided solely by your intuitive and animal parts. Let this movement unfurling within you guide your steps. You will also begin to feel the need to return to your inner world and may be less inclined to exchange or interact with others. Instead you start to look deeper inside yourself. This call will become increasingly powerful until the next New Moon.

This is a period of sorting, cleansing sacred spaces, and taking a thorough look at your current situation. You may use this force to rid yourself of negative influences, weights, and blockages that are holding you back. Trust your instincts in order to leave behind whatever encumbers you: relationships, mental patterns, habits, and repetitive life schemas. You can make mindful choices, banish what no longer serves you, and close certain chapters in your life before heading into a new cycle.

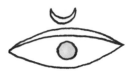

○ LUNAR TERMINOLOGY

Depending on her position and her "color," the Moon has a variety of designations that together form a specific terminology. It is worth being familiar with this terminology because it reveals the Moon's influences over us.

ASCENDING AND DESCENDING MOON

When the Moon is ascending or descending, this does not mean that she is waxing or waning. The Moon changes position in the sky and moves closer to or farther away from Earth. To determine whether she is ascending or descending, you must observe her movement around a fixed point (a church tower, the top of a tree, the roof of a building) for several days. Sometimes you will see that she comes closer to the point you selected; in this case she is descending. At other times she moves farther away; this means she is ascending. The Moon can, therefore, be ascending and waning or descending and waxing.

LUNAR NODES

Earth turns around the Sun on what is known as the "ecliptic" plane. As the Moon turns around the Earth, she intersects with this plane twice during her orbit. These intersections are the lunar nodes. The "ascending node" in the North is called the "head of the dragon" and the "descending node" in the South is the "tail of the dragon." The Moon needs just over 27 days to make her way around the dragon before returning to the North node. In karmic astrology and its study of our past lives, these nodes have meaning. The North node corresponds to your current life path and the South node represents your karmic experiences and the lessons you can draw from them. Every 18½ years, these nodes find themselves in the same position as the day you were born. In terms of your personal development, each return to this position corresponds to stages in your life that are decisive passages in your existence, large portals that close and open cycles: ages 18–19, ages 36–37, age 55, ages 73–74, and age 92. These periods can be broken down into smaller cycles of nine years when the North and South nodes invert their positions (age 9, age 27, age 45, age 63, age 81, age 99).

PERIGEE

The Moon's orbit is shaped like an ellipse, not a circle, so the distance between Earth and the Moon varies. The perigee is the moment when the Moon is closest to the Earth. This is also when her effects have a greater influence on us.

APOGEE

This is the point in the Moon's elliptical orbit when she is farthest away from Earth.

SUPERMOON

This phenomenon takes place when the perigee period is very short and the Moon is therefore closer than usual to Earth. This can be observed with the naked eye during a Full Moon when the Moon looks particularly large and bright. This is always a time when lunar energies are considerably strong. Another extremely rare phenomenon occurs when the Moon comes close to the Earth before its usual perigee. This is known as an Ultimate Moon. Only twenty Ultimate Moons have been recorded during the Christian era and the most recent was in 1912.

ECLIPSE

This takes place during the Full Moon when the Sun, Earth, and Moon are in perfect alignment. The Moon passes into the Earth's shadow and no longer receives the Sun's light. This phenomenon happens twice a year in the form of partial eclipses, but total eclipses are rarer and have stronger effects. Symbolically, the eclipse represents the revelation of what is hidden. The moment you dive into your depths, your innerness, to reveal your authenticity and bring to the surface what has been buried, you bare the darker parts of you that are usually kept in the shadows and this becomes a space of transformation. Total eclipses are rare and will push you to work on your relationships with blood relatives, your spouse, family, and clan. In energetic terms, eclipses are sources of emotional upheaval, restlessness, and tension. They are a passage from dark to light and a renovation to balance out what you choose to leave behind as you move toward your future.

BLUE MOON

The Blue Moon is a rare phenomenon and is the name given to the second Full Moon in a month. Her presence indicates to us that we are in a year of thirteen Moons. The number thirteen has taken on its superstitious symbolism because of this link to the Moon. The second Full Moon has the same energetic characteristics as the first but she is more powerful and her influences are amplified. She crafts our spiritual energies.

BLACK MOON

The New Moon is commonly called the Black Moon because she is veiled and does not provide any light. The term is also used when there are two New Moons in the same month. Like the Blue Moon (the second Full Moon in the month), the Black Moon brings a surplus of energy. She supports psychological work, meditation, and divination.

This term is also found in karmic astrology to describe an intangible point in the empty focus of the Moon's orbit that is in the sky when each of us is born. It is another detail from your birth chart that can provide a wealth of information.

WHITE MOON

This is another name for the Full Moon.

PINK MOON OR SPROUTING GRASS MOON

This is the first Full Moon after Easter, usually between mid-April and mid-May. It is not necessarily pink, contrary to what most people believe, but is symbolic of the farmer's fear: if the Full Moon is visible in a clear sky, the risk of frost is greater and the first shoots that come out of the Earth could burn. People may also refer to the Pink Moon during eclipses or when the Moon is low on the horizon and takes on an orange color.

RED MOON

The two days before and after the Full Moon.

ASH MOON

This is the name given to the two days that precede and follow the New Moon. The color of the sky takes on an ash grey color because of the weak light.

BLOOD MOON

This name comes from the Moon's appearance during total eclipses. When she does not receive sunlight directly, she becomes bathed in a reddish color before passing into earthly darkness. Energies are multiplied tenfold and may at times cause restlessness and difficulty settling your mind and body.

CONNECTING TO THE MOON

There is a story being woven between you and the Moon and it's time to start writing it down. Open your soul and set your feelings down on paper. Take pleasure in creating a moon journal that reflects who you are. This journal will become your traveling companion. Then, put together a calendar recording your female cycles. It will become your map of the sky. Finally, allow the magic of the night to live within you. As you open yourself to the world of dreams, draw your dream circle. Each of these creative tools will become your work instrument: something personalized, just right, that will help you tell the story of your transformation, your path, and your lunar journey.

○ MOON JOURNAL

The moon journal is the place where, when it feels right, you will make a note of the bridges that exist between your life (feelings, inspirations, synchronicities, physical states) and the Moon. This is an intimate space that should feel like it belongs to you as you mindfully seek the path to your true nature. As you keep this journal you will see connections between energy fluctuations and your inner activity. You can then apply the rhythm that feels right to use in your daily life. Don't hesitate to dive in and invest in a journal with thick pages so you can paint, glue things in, or draw if you want to.

Using any of the lunar calendars that are widely available on the Internet, first write down the following, month by month:

- The phases of the Moon, the date, NM for New Moon or FM for Full Moon, and drawings of the first and last quarter;
- Lunar and astronomical events such as an eclipse or supermoon;
- The position of the Moon in the planets: FM in Sagittarius, NM in Cancer, etc.

You can enrich this basic structure with personal events, dates that are meaningful to you, the position of the Moon in your birth chart, significant events, or pagan festivals.

Enter into the creative and personal part of yourself where you can record your feelings, the lunar energies emitted month after month, and the integration of your own rituals with those that are offered in this book.

Write down your intentions during each Black Moon and all the things you are grateful for during each White Moon. Be attentive to what happens within you when the Full Moon reappears in your moon sign.

Your journal is also a reference resource. You can write down things you read, quotations, or songs that inspire you and connect you to the Moon.

You can certainly fill your journal with words, but you can also use all forms of artistic expression to express this connection (drawing, collage, photography). Feel free and creative. Have fun! Let this journal be a reflection of your imagination and personality!

○ MENSTRUAL CYCLE CALENDAR

Recording your menstrual cycle on a calendar will help you follow and learn to live with your flows and emotional and creative undulations. With each passing month you will better understand how you function and will discover your phases of creativity, withdrawal, innerness, the moments when you are fully available to others vs. those when you need to recenter yourself, and active periods vs. those that are more intuitive. By becoming familiar with your own rhythm (which is the rhythm of no other woman) and juggling these different moments in your daily life, you will be able to reach your fullest potential. Schedule meetings at certain times that might be better than others. Use your creative awakening at the best time of the month. Prioritize your inner life over collective activities depending upon these energies. Know how to say no when you have to.

Your only task is to make the best calendar for you. Fill it with your personality, honor this intimate listening, and allow the creative part of you to express itself in this personal space.

Begin this calendar on the first day of your cycle, D1. Note the date and record the following:

- Physical sensations (pain, fatigue, well-being);
- Emotions (anger, boredom, joy, serenity);

SET INTENTIONS -
PURIFICATION

NEW MOON

CLEAN -
SORT

BEGIN -
SELF-CARE -
CREATE

CLOSING
CHAPTERS

OPEN YOURSELF -
ORGANIZE -
ACT

GRATITUDE TO
SELF

GRATITUDE
TO
OTHERS

FULL MOON

RECHARGE YOUR
ENERGIES, STONES,
MAGICAL TOOLS

- Needs (to be alone, desire to create, to stay home, to sleep);
- Intuitions;
- Sex drive;
- Desires (to eat, to wear, etc.)—these may seem like details, but everything means something.

Continue doing this every day (often between 26 and 29 days) until your next cycle begins and you return to D1. Month by month you will see how your energies take shape.

○ DREAM CIRCLE

I inherited my ability to connect with the dream universe from my grandmother. She used to have prophetic dreams and this led me to ask questions about this power from an early age. She called women "dreamers" because of our capacity to "see" messages about the past, present, and future and to visit other people in our dreams. It wasn't until much later that I discovered women on the other side of the world had experienced the same things as my grandmother and used the same practices. In the Native American tradition this aptitude was linked to the Moon and the uterus was seen as the crucible of dreams. Dreams represent silk threads that stretch from our womb to the Moon, connecting us to her. This is what is called "dream weaving." For me, this "weaving" appears in the form of a harp that can be played by connecting to it physically, emotionally, and spiritually to develop intuitive capabilities.

The dream circle will allow you to explore the content of your dreams and establish a relationship between the lunar cycles and your personal cycles. When you transcribe your dreams, you will make startling discoveries and notice recurrent themes that correlate with the Moon's passing through certain signs. You will find that for 2½ days each month, when the Moon returns to the position she had when you were born—in your moon sign, in other words—her influence over you is more powerful. The symbols that emerge may be the fruit of analysis, evocation, or inspiration. Allow yourself to be guided by your sensations and visions and use myths, tales, and archetypes to interpret your dreams and unite your experience with universal and ancestral knowledge.

To create a dream circle, draw a circle and divide it into thirty sections.

On the first day of your menstrual cycle, write down the date, the Moon's position in the zodiac, and the Moon phase. Then, note the themes that come up in your dreams, the symbols that appear, and any emotions that are present. If needed, you can expand your story outside of the dream circle on a separate sheet of paper to explore the framework in greater depth and record key moments, places, people, animals you encountered, and other details.

Keep your journal and dream circle nearby at night, and when you wake up in the morning, write down what comes to mind immediately before you reenter full consciousness.

Working through your dreams is a practice that can be honed over time. When you go in search of your interior world, you no longer dream and instead "are dreamed." Your visions give you information about your life as well as messages of a more collective nature. Each woman who chooses to commit to this path will discover the infinite possibilities that it carries. In the next part of this book, we will discover the major dream themes associated with each zodiac constellation.

THE MAGIC OF
THE ZODIAC

Being part of a great All implies turning ourselves toward the cosmos. We cannot ignore that what is taking place in the sky has an impact on our existence. Every constellation and every planet is a string that stretches between us and connects us; astrology allows us to hear the music of these strings and is in fact an attempt to represent the world. Each time the Moon enters a sign, she uses energetic resonance to invite us to question and understand a piece of our existence. Without fear and with respect, you too can claim these celestial spaces, decode their influences, and use them as tools to refine your inner journey. We will now discover how astrology infuses our lives.

○ THE MOON AND YOUR BIRTH CHART

The twelve signs of the zodiac have twelve different energies that represent twelve different ways of interpreting the world. What happens in the sky has an effect on Earth. The Moon influences you all the time, but in personal, nuanced ways because of your sign and the simple fact that we are all different people. Tropical astrology is based on the position of the Sun and is the form of astrology the Western world is most familiar with. While many of us know our sun sign, now that we are aware of the Moon's impact on our lives it's worth discovering her place in our horoscope. If you don't know your moon sign, there are many websites today that can provide this information for free. Once you know your sign it will be interesting to see what happens in your life when the Moon returns to the position she was in the moment you were born. If your sun sign is Scorpio, for example, she will return to this position every 29.5 days and at that moment her influence over you is greatest.

If you are interested in knowing the Moon's position in the sky each day, there are sites and mobile applications that can help you find her easily. The Sun moves more slowly and spends around thirty days in each sign while the Moon passes through a different sign every two or three days. During her cycle, she always follows the same order on the zodiac wheel: Aries, Taurus, Gemini, Cancer, Leo, Virgo, Libra, Scorpio, Sagittarius, Capricorn, Aquarius, Pisces.

It is especially interesting to observe where the Moon is situated during the two moments each month that carry the greatest energy: the Full Moon (which I talk about in greater detail here because she is highly influential) and the New Moon.

The moon signs are divided into three categories: cardinal signs, fixed signs, and mutable signs.

The cardinal signs are the signs at the entrance to each season: Aries, Cancer, Libra, and Capricorn. They represent beginnings and are bearers of intention. They move with their gaze fixed on the future, showing which direction to follow. Their energies are linked to action, communication, and authority.

The fixed signs, Taurus, Leo, Scorpio, and Aquarius, are each located at the peak of a season and are its guardians. Their role is often to go in a specific direction, a life path that they will not deviate from. As a result, they sometimes seem a little rigid to the rest of the world and those who do not adhere as intensely to their principles. The energies of these signs are root-building, willpower, and stability.

The mutable signs are Gemini, Virgo, Sagittarius, and Pisces. They close the season and are founded on change and evolution. Their energies are linked to rebirth, movement, and reflection.

When you look for the constellation the Moon is passing through, you should also look for what sign the Sun is in. This yin-yang axis functions by responding to a balance of forces just like everything else. The observations you make in your moon journal come from the Sky to lead you to your inner lands. They will show you how the Moon interacts with you.

○ **THE FULL MOON IN EACH CONSTELLATION, WITH ITS DREAM CIRCLE**

FULL MOON IN ARIES: ACTION

When the Moon is in Aries you are pushed to action, and she asks you to clearly set your intentions for the goals you hope to achieve. She guides you toward the paths to take that will bring your plans to fruition at the following New Moon.

If unguided, the energy that inhabits you during this time will turn against you. Ask the Moon to welcome, calm, and help you. If you let yourself be guided you will be able to become a creator and pioneer in your areas of expertise. She will bring you the boldness and determination needed to realize your deepest desires. Believe in your ability to channel this powerful energy and leave anger to the side, fighting against impulsivity. You know where you are going, so why risk ruining everything by acting too quickly? Be like the ram, anchored to the earth while nourishing your inner fire.

Aries dream circle: coming to awareness. The dreams that come to you when the Moon is in Aries are powerful. They speak to a part of you that you often try to keep under control. They are linked to changes you would like to put in place now, breaking with your past. They may reveal an unconscious resistance and a need to rethink certain aspects of your life.

FULL MOON IN TAURUS: INCARNATION IN MATTER

When the Moon comes to nest in the Taurus constellation, a fixed Earth sign, she is speaking to you about the way you incarnate your spirituality in physical matter. She reveals your mystical dimension and authenticity. It is a time to understand where you are in your personal fulfillment. Take stock of the harvests you have reaped for months or years inside of you and contemplate the path you have taken, congratulating yourself on the work you have accomplished. If your foundations are solid, let your soul be like that of a messenger: it is time to pass something on to others. This may be an opportunity to organize long-term projects, reach out to others, collaborate, and take your rightful place on this path of sharing. Be careful: the "mastery" you apply to your life must not become a form of "control," and your relationships with others must not become possessive bonds. Reject the temptation to impose your values on other people. The powerful action force of the Full Moon in Taurus, slow but full of tenacity, must be used in service of the beauty of life.

Taurus dream circle: Sky–Earth harmony. In the Taurus constellation you will channel dreams connected to nature and its power, perhaps in the form of storms or earthquakes. These dreams also speak about your elevation upward, words revealing your inner beauty, and singing as a path to elevation.

FULL MOON IN GEMINI: THE RIGHT WORD

When the Moon is in Gemini she points toward your relationships with others. She reminds you that not everything is black or white, bad or good. Sometimes you speak too quickly, putting yourself in an uncomfortable situation, or are swept up by emotional tides that you cannot control. To make it through the storm you will need clarity, and this requires that you take the time to think about your rapport with the Other. Geminis represent two sides of the same soul: one side in the light, the other in darkness. They may also be seen as a symbol of evolution, a pouring out of the self in order to move in the direction of the person facing us. Under this Moon you will have to grow in maturity and scratch to see what is hidden beneath your need to be present for others. Is it authentic? Is it measured? Are you multiplying your number of contacts for the right reasons? What are you looking for in the flow of words that have been pouring out of you for the past few days? The Moon encourages you to find what is appropriate for you and the other person and to question yourself about how you communicate and share your values. You may find that some relationships seem to have lost their meaning, strength, or goodwill, or perhaps the exchange you thought was enriching was in fact simply sought out as a response to your need to be valued. This awareness may make you feel scattered because you are not sure how to rebalance these bonds. Before doing anything, you must recenter yourself, slow down, and take time for inner silence in order to return to a better form of communication and a more sincere radiance in your relationships. The decisions you make now will be the right ones because they are dictated by a concern for honesty and no longer by the ego.

Gemini dream circle: communication. Dreams in this sign are linked to joy, the fear of living, or your ability to understand life. They may reveal a situation in which you are suffocating, lacking freedom, or in which your territory is being invaded. They also involve communication and exchange. Like Gemini, these dreams reflect the two facets of your personality and act as a mirror between your unconscious and conscious selves by transferring messages that connect the two sides.

FULL MOON IN CANCER: SENSITIVITY

When the Moon travels through this constellation she is entering her domain. Cancer is a Water sign and resonates with the energies of the Moon, whose influence unfurls freely because she is "at home" in this sign: this period features a rich inner life, powerful dreams, increased sensitivity, and emotions that run through you like a river. Your sensitive world is given priority, as are the people who are part of it: your family and friends. This Moon works on your alignment, your verticality, and your positioning between the Earth and Sky. This is not some kind of rigid rod, but simply a flexible silver thread that navigates between two worlds, past and present. You are surrounded by mystery. Your intuition is at work, so allow it to express itself. Become a she-wolf, a nurturing and empathetic protector of your offspring. Be careful, though, not to let your emotions overflow, and pay attention to your hypersensitivity. If you fall victim to these rollercoasters it is probably because you are unable to place limits on them. Your strong capacity for compassion needs to be counterbalanced so you don't become exhausted after dispersing too much energy. You will have to find an equilibrium between the will to be present for others in a generous and altruistic way and your need to revitalize and protect yourself from destabilizing external influences.

Cancer dream circle: intimacy. These dreams are associated with your interiority and, therefore, with your creativity. They talk about fertility, the couple, and the home. You may dream about a house; perhaps it is the one you grew up in or perhaps it is somewhere by the sea, surrounded by immense waves. These themes symbolize security and emotions.

FULL MOON IN LEO: RADIANCE

This Moon inspires and unveils you, putting you at the center of the circle. Pushed by your solar yang, you come onto the playing field to shine. You are able to reveal your personal power thanks to a creative energy that is in expansion and an unbridled imagination. Dream big and note that this period is suited to flourishing and joy-filled projects that go in the direction of your destiny. Subtle energies are powerful and may be precious allies, but you will have to channel them to avoid falling into the trap of tyranny or stubbornness.

Work on reuniting, not dividing. Watch out for your tendency to impose your points of view on others and to model your way of functioning after that of other people. Look at each situation from above so you can take a step back without risking a needless waste of energy. If you can navigate this turn carefully, this is a time filled with encounters and exciting connections. This Moon invites you to be an independent and powerful lioness, protective of your clan and your ideals.

Leo dream circle: relationships. The dreams that are born from this constellation are exhilarating. They concern you directly and may include images of your presence at collective gatherings. They reveal your unconscious projections, your true nature, and your need for freedom. They speak about your roots.

FULL MOON IN VIRGO: INDEPENDENCE

This Full Moon can be destabilizing because despite its "anchored" nature and apparent stability, it can sometimes be a source of anxiety. You may find it difficult to allow your thoughts to coexist with your material projects. Be careful not to let your mind become resistant and don't allow yourself to feel scattered because you will be quickly submerged by the list of tasks to complete. It is essential not to let your limiting thoughts run in a loop and make you feel like a victim. Be careful not to lose control out of a lack of flexibility. Under this Moon it is easier to reinforce your anchoring to the Earth, which will help you avoid getting carried away by the flow of your thoughts. Put down your roots, settle yourself in your home to get your bearings, and put everything on pause. If you can handle this difficult period with suppleness, you will earn the freedom that is characteristic of this lunar influence and Virgo, the virgin, will reclaim its ancient definition: a woman of experience who is free in her decisions, free in her sexuality—which does not belong to a father or husband—and in charge of her own destiny. She nourishes your quest for independence and your relationship with the Sky and Earth. She asks you to connect to something greater and to develop your spirituality through concrete rituals that are performed mindfully and shared with your clan.

Virgo dream circle: healing. The dreams born when the Moon is under Virgo are often brimming with details. They abound with concrete information that you can use in your incarnate life to get organized and make decisions.

Dreams in Virgo are also related to healing and contain teachings that will help you treat your wounds, particularly when they are linked to the body.

FULL MOON IN LIBRA: HARMONY

We tend to oscillate under the effects of this Moon because, while she is characterized by balance, she nevertheless shows us how difficult it can be to find it. Your thoughts will focus on what is preoccupying you in the present: your romantic relationships, first and foremost, but also those with your friends and colleagues. Find the point of equilibrium to bring these relationships into harmony with each other. Unfortunately, this is no easy task because this Moon causes significant emotional upheaval. Your emotions will collide with your thinking mind in waves. The trick is to listen to your reason rather than your passion. Control your sensations and focus on trusting what seems right to you even if it goes against your immediate desires. Learn to see further ahead. Welcome what comes without forcing destiny; test your stoicism. What will happen will happen. Establish a bond between the heart and reason; between the two is the correct path that will help you achieve harmony.

Libra dream circle: the inner child. When the Moon travels through Libra, dreams center on your deepest nature, your emotional bonds, and your inner child. They are associated with the mother and with intimacy. They speak to you about your verticality and your ability to eliminate negative emotions. They also give you indications about your equilibrium.

FULL MOON IN SCORPIO: INSTINCT

The powerful energies of this Moon call to you fervently and connect you to your mystery, spirituality, and sexual power. You receive these energies directly. Water, this sign's element, favors strong and profound emotions. This Full Moon encourages you to shed your skin, abandon your old rags, and purify yourself. This can lead to emotivity, restlessness, and even a certain form of depression. It brings things to the surface that you had buried deep inside, which can be unpleasant if you allow it to happen but if you can get beyond your fears there is a radical spiritual change at work. This is the moment to let your intuition speak and to develop it further by using divination tools like tarot cards or pendulums. This Full Moon connects you to your deepest instincts and is well-suited to intense spiritual experiences like shamanic journeys and sacred sexuality practices such as tantra and kundalini awakening.

These practices are helpful for blending spirituality and sexual power. **Scorpion dream circle: revelation.** These dreams are deep, reveal what is hidden, and dig up the unconscious. They may be linked to sexuality, death, and transformation. They concern your sensations and the part of you concerned with lucidity and discernment.

FULL MOON IN SAGITTARIUS: LISTENING TO THE BODY

The arrows of Sagittarius point us in a direction; they show us the path— and not the end of it. This Moon pushes you to move forward, to keep your objective in mind, and to remember that your evolution is found not in a sense of finality but in the path that lies ahead of you. She asks you to watch over yourself by putting the brakes on your tendency toward fragmentation; this inclination is characteristic of Sagittarius but leads you to unnecessarily multiply your fields of interest. The Moon prompts you instead to rebuild your strength before taking any kind of action and to touch upon your truth. This is the only worthwhile way to continue your initiation. She encourages you to persevere in your exploration of spiritual dimensions and links thought to movement: when the first is clear and right, she will bring about the second. Under the sign of teaching this Moon encourages you to continue quenching your thirst for learning because this will make you a steady and knowledgeable guide. This Moon also speaks of independence, which in this case is more than another word for solitude. On the contrary, this independence offers you a chance to align the power of your own freedom with an authentic sharing of your feelings and values with other people. The act of listening to the body also dominates under this Moon because it can help reveal things you do not perceive or do not necessarily want to see. Your body is your house, the place you restore yourself, and your temple. When you dedicate yourself to it by massaging it, unfolding it, and reading its messages, you can better understand and view your being as a whole. This in turn will reinforce your holistic relationship with the Earth, where the Sagittarius anchors his hoofs, and the Sky, toward which he points his bow.

Sagittarius dream circle: premonition. Dreams may take on a prophetic quality because they are linked to the future. They focus on family bonds and speak about commitment, strength, and courage. They may also be connected to your relationship with your body.

FULL MOON IN CAPRICORN: CONSTRUCTION

This is the Moon of builders and architects and emits a very yang energy. You need to question your foundations and dissect the way you function. You may have projects in mind—significant long-term commitments, intentions for the next few months—but you don't always ask yourself about the foundation upon which you are going to construct yourself. As a result, your potential and your flaws fall through the holes in the sieve of reality. Take a serious look at your desires and what is possible for you. You may have to isolate yourself to conduct this introspective analysis. Enter this phase of reflection and begin the process of deprogramming and reprogramming your life. It is an ambitious procedure aimed at cleaning out—in depth—the things you have buried in order to program new elements aligned with your personal evolution. This process is accompanied by an intense energetic cleansing. Accept the time needed for this work and do not decide anything impulsively; when you undertake this cleansing, the cards are often reshuffled and you end up taking unexpected paths.

Capricorn dream circle: quintessence. In this constellation, dreams symbolize death and rebirth. They speak about your deep internal structure, your nature, and your essence. They may be connected to your real or symbolic family and might concern issues of territory. They are linked to bones, skin, teeth, and nails.

FULL MOON IN AQUARIUS: LIBERTY

This Moon gives you permission to take responsibility for what is holding you back and to detach yourself from what others think about you. You can be the woman you want to be; you can be nonconformist and independent. Liberate yourself from what is superfluous and what you do not need. Return to the essential values that bring you together with other people, and take steps into and alongside your community. Under this Moon you leave your apprenticeship to put what you have learned into practice. You will be able to access a collective consciousness that is aimed at a higher goal. You are asked to look after your liberty while remembering that this freedom has no meaning unless you share what you know with the people around you. You have to be at once inside and outside the circle. With this Moon's influence you will break with a distant past that has programmed part of your life and no longer belongs in it. Be aware of the things you have learned and know that they will enrich your future more than you ever thought possible. Knowing this, lean on these solid foundations to launch your future projects.

Aquarius dream circle: change. Your dreams acquire a unique emotional texture during this time. They reveal changes for yourself and others, upheavals, and at times you may encounter natural disasters, which are synonyms for our internal disorders. These dreams also speak about your way of communicating and can be prophetic.

FULL MOON IN PISCES: THE ART OF THE DREAM

This Moon will prove to you that the possibilities within you are limitless. She binds you to your inner rivers. It is time to dive into those deep waters: allow yourself to gently float and visualize yourself coasting down this internal river, discovering all of the joys it contains. This Moon stirs up your emotional center and brings many feelings to the surface without sorting through them. You may be confronted with difficult emotions. You will need to find a peaceful place, a refuge, a circle where you can safely settle your feelings. This Moon in Pisces is a privileged time for you to reconnect with your deepest "me," step back from the flow of daily life, and honor your interior wealth. This period is characterized by the presence of dreams. These may be awakened in the form of aspirations or when your guides and subconscious speak to you in your sleep. Open yourself to this channel of intangible communication that has brought guidance, counsel, and healing since the dawn of humanity. You may not be able to detect specific messages but you can still connect to the emotions of these dreams and be grateful for this precious conversation, for it feeds your soul and takes care of you.

Pisces dream circle: the unconscious. The Moon is growing stronger and connects directly with your unconscious. Your dreams will arouse many emotions. They will be fluid and clear and will deliver messages of wisdom to you as well as divinations about your loved ones. These dreams reference water as a link to abundance and fertility. They may also involve running away, racing, a road to travel, or a quest to carry out.

THE MEMORY OF
THE BLACK MOON

The Black Moon is an extraordinary instrument for reading the soul. It is an imaginary point in our astrological birth chart that was rebaptized as "Lilith" in the 1970s in reference to Adam's mythical first lover, who symbolized transgression and a threat to equilibrium. Understanding the Black Moon opens us to the possibility of past lives because she speaks to us about our karmic past. She points us to a moment in our past existence that was our downfall. Equilibrium is being reestablished in the lives that follow this error, and you can construct yourself in opposition to the primal fear that caused your fall: this reconstruction is known as the Priapus. We will interpret each Black Moon in correspondence with a past life, and each Priapus as the current state of affairs in our present life. We will consider the Black Moon as the dominant feature of a past that is unknown to us but nevertheless pushes us to take certain actions in our current incarnation.

Revealing your Black Moon can be unsettling because it represents a somber and unconscious zone within you. Unveiling it floods these darker parts of you with light and helps you understand who you are and how you can work on certain imbalances. The Black Moon is your original node and opens your eyes to the source of your own ruin, but by forcing you to confront your greatest fears she helps you begin a powerful healing process. We all have a sign containing our Black Moon and an online birth chart should be able to calculate the location of this point for you. In this chapter I am offering an interpretation for each sign, but be sure to keep in mind the chart as a whole.

○ BLACK MOON IN ARIES—PRIAPUS IN LIBRA:
VIOLENCE VS HARMONY

The Black Moon in Aries possesses a fiery energy that is linked to Mars, the god of war. Your founding myth is that of the warrior who allowed himself to be overtaken by his desire for revenge and became a bloodthirsty animal. Your outbursts became uncontrollable. You were a tyrant, you acted violently and impulsively, and this brutality turned against you physically. For this reason, there may be traces of unconscious memories involving fear of bladed weapons, fire, and rape.

YOUR GREATEST FEAR as the Black Moon in Aries is violence, and you dread every form of aggression, competition, and rejection by others.

PRIAPUS IN LIBRA: You are building a universe of softness, beauty, and balance. You take the time to think and measure your actions and words. Aestheticism is paramount because it removes you from the universe of the conquering and ferocious creature. You seek to please in order to be accepted and want to show how beautiful the world can be even in the midst of chaos. You are very yin and are honing your ability to listen to and embrace others.

○ BLACK MOON IN TAURUS—PRIAPUS IN SCORPIO: DEPENDENCY VS INFLEXIBILITY

The Black Moon in Taurus reveals capacities for construction worthy of an architect. You successfully completed a series of solid and ambitious projects that were intended to help you make significant material gains. You savored the benefits you reaped and your need to possess transformed into a fear of loss that eventually paralyzed you and prevented you from taking action or evolving. You closed yourself off so you could accumulate material and human possessions and jealousy and dependency became your downfall.

YOUR GREATEST FEAR is losing what you have and being dependent on a person or substance.

PRIAPUS IN SCORPIO brings you willpower and energy, along with an ethical sense that is so pronounced it verges on the despotic. Your primal fear from your past life makes you view money as taboo. It is impossible for you to accumulate wealth because you squander it or give it away. You have developed a rather rigid morality and as a result demonstrate inflexibility toward those around you.

○ BLACK MOON IN GEMINI—PRIAPUS IN SAGITTARIUS: MANIPULATION VS SINCERITY

The Black Moon in Gemini represents both a search for knowledge and a love of communication. You were an expert at shining in society, but to make sure you were always winning you had to lie and adopted a manipulative way of speaking: this is the downfall of this sign.

YOUR GREATEST FEAR is not being listened to, making mistakes, or not having the right words or discourse to captivate your audience. You have a tendency to develop respiratory problems because the throat, a symbol of communication, is the door to the lungs.

PRIAPUS IN SAGITTARIUS opens you to sincerity, simplicity, outspokenness, and sometimes even naivety. Something you say might go too far but you are quick to put your own overzealousness in check. You open yourself to others through your humanist values and perceive the best in everyone, so much so that you are sometimes blind to people's faults.

○ BLACK MOON IN CANCER—PRIAPUS IN CAPRICORN: SUFFOCATION VS RATIONALISM

The Black Moon in Cancer represents the archetypal mother and everything she brings to mind: gentleness, the ability to care for others, and devotion to one's family or people in distress. In your past life you surrounded, secured, nourished, and cuddled others to a fault. With limitless self-sacrifice you aspired to fusion in your relationships and erected golden cages around the people you loved. Because of your desire to give too much, you suffocated other people and these relationships abruptly ended.

YOUR GREATEST FEAR is linked to everything that resembles the family environment in one form or another. You reject all feminine energy and are obsessively afraid of losing physical control of your body. You may notice problems connected to eating and digestion.

PRIAPUS IN CAPRICORN arrives to set limits and create a framework. You rigorously respect rules and laws and rationalize everything, even human relationships. Your individual space is powerful enough that you do not need others and you run from any kind of dependency. A certain softness often seems to be lacking in this rigorous approach to living, but it is still there, carefully tucked away. The slightest display of sentimentality, however, would be a demonstration of unacceptable weakness. Be open to showing a little bit of this softness because it is, after all, your essence.

○ BLACK MOON IN LEO—PRIAPUS IN AQUARIUS: PRIDE VS RETREAT

The Black Moon in Leo marks an indisputable radiance. You were a charismatic being and the center of everyone's attention. People watched everything you did with interest. You had nothing to prove and this is

what led to your fall. Persuaded that you had it all, you became dispro-
portionately proud and stopped tolerating opinions contrary to your own
and even the slightest departure from your mindset. This is the behavior
that provoked your humiliating tumble from your pedestal.

YOUR GREATEST FEAR is being in the shadows: you can't bear being
in second place and no longer being admired and would prefer to pull
away completely. You withdraw. You sometimes encounter joint problems, forms of rheumatism, and photosensitivity.

PRIAPUS IN AQUARIUS completely counterbalances your fear of being
in the spotlight. Leo's greatness will help you contribute to ambitious
group projects that will have an impact on the entire community. You are
innovative and add value to these projects, but the shadow of omnipo-
tence may reemerge when you try to impose your vision on others under
the guise of great humanist principles. You are characterized by your
ability to live with others but outside the circle. On the other hand, you
are captivated by sunny personalities that capture other people's attention and whose radiance is so powerful that it splashes over onto you.

○ BLACK MOON IN VIRGO—PRIAPUS IN PISCES: STUBBORNNESS VS INDIFFERENCE

The Black Moon in Virgo engenders a profound desire to attain per-
fection. Your creativity pushed you to explore areas that required total
commitment, and you knew exactly what to do. This concern for absolute purity had another side, though: it was a kind of rigor that made
you become stubborn in your opinions. Your universe became filled with
details and small worries and reduced itself to a small circle. The light-
ness disappeared. You couldn't bear acknowledging a single one of your
weaknesses or errors and so you adopted a victim stance. You became
rigid, hard, and imprisoned yourself in a miniscule life.

YOUR GREATEST FEAR is any form of shackles or yoke. The personalities of people born under this Moon often have symptoms such as intes-
tinal problems, allergies, feelings of suffocation, and sometimes asthma.

PRIAPUS IN PISCES develops a universe with blurred edges; its contours
are always moving and you straddle the two sides of this river, enjoying letting yourself be carried along by the current. You are following
your instinct. What you desire to maintain in this life is the absence of a

framework. You are open, tolerant—sometimes too much so—and your own limits are violated when you become unrestrictedly available to others. There is a risk that you may forget yourself behind these constantly open doors, these endless moments of listening and being present for another person. People call you devoted, kind-hearted, and sometimes say, unfortunately, that you willingly allow yourself to be exploited.

○ BLACK MOON IN LIBRA—PRIAPUS IN ARIES: APATHY VS ACTION

The Black Moon in Libra represents the quest for beauty. You enjoyed being surrounded by people who vied for your attention or a smile in their direction and praised your sensitivity and artistic taste. You enjoyed the gifts life gave you because all you had to do to get them was reach out your hand. Your downfall was born out of this vanity. You lost the desire to exert effort and instead lived off of your wealth. You loafed around and eventually someone else acted in your place. Guided by easy pleasure, you allowed yourself to slide little by little into an apathy that made you completely dependent on others.

YOUR GREATEST FEAR is rejection by the person you love. Romantic relationships are demanding and you live in constant fear of being abandoned, so you settle for toxic substances and people. Physical addiction may be present.

PRIAPUS IN ARIES uses this sign's fire to stir up action wherever possible. You run away from nonchalant personalities and any situation involving dependency. You live for being a catalyst, never hesitating before investing yourself in a project and giving your time and energy. Other people appreciate this overflowing energy, this outspokenness and its power to move mountains. You keep your visceral fear of being rejected by the one you love buried deep within. It takes a lot of time and confidence in the other person for you to invest in a relationship. Any sensation of emotional dependency will make you leave, so you have to find a balance between freedom and construction for it to work.

○ BLACK MOON IN SCORPIO—PRIAPUS IN TAURUS: ENSLAVEMENT VS ANCHORING

The Black Moon in Scorpio made you an enigmatic being. Your charisma, your exceptional ability to connect to the invisible world, and your extraordinary psychological capacities made you shamans, witches, or healers in your communities. Magic, the esoteric world, and your pursuit of the cycle of life always pushed you to go further, sometimes even to the point of enslaving your "disciples." The downfall of this Black Moon unfolds in this dark area: using seduction, desire, and psychological finesse, you manipulated other people to preserve your own upward movement.

YOUR GREATEST FEAR is connected to the people you abused on your karmic path. Now you are haunted by the fear of being manipulated.

PRIAPUS IN TAURUS will develop an immutable force, stability, and honesty. You keep your distance from any kind of manipulation and mystification and have a natural gift for listening and intuition that you use to serve others. This Black Moon is the most deeply rooted of all the signs, vibrates in rhythm with the Earth, and motivates you to defend your planet. Your willingness to improve life and make the world a better place prompts you to create projects that bring people together without putting yourself at the forefront. Your lively spirit is greatly admired but you sometimes wear yourself out because you have a hard time saying no. Your fidelity is indisputable, unwavering, and without any ulterior motive. You protect yourself from devious people.

○ BLACK MOON IN SAGITTARIUS—PRIAPUS IN GEMINI: MYSTICISM VS RATIONALITY

The Black Moon in Sagittarius evokes a personality of strong ideals and relentless questioning of the self about life and the divine. You were driven by a humanist vision and put all of your energy into the transmission of wisdom. Your faith pushed you to assume the role of enlightened guide, but after looking into the mystical depths you lost all concept of reality and self-criticism. While you were once a charismatic mentor, you became a despot, giving in to your need to be loved and followed unconditionally. But the wheel turned and those who used to sing your praises now want to throw stones at you.

YOUR GREATEST FEAR is a lack of social recognition and not being able to find your place within a community. Physically, the legs are the weakest area.

PRIAPUS IN GEMINI builds a person rich in knowledge who knows how to share with discernment. You are rational, communicative, open, and hungry to learn and pass on what you know in the right context. You rely on what is tangible and visible. You avoid people who speak too much or too loudly. When you have some distance from these troublesome personalities you enjoy building your own small realm of tolerance that is open to the world.

○ BLACK MOON IN CAPRICORN—PRIAPUS IN CANCER: CONTEMPT VS KINDNESS

The Black Moon in Capricorn reveals that you were once a great sage who embodied seriousness, study, and reason. You were intelligent and erudite and had a difficult time with people who chose to question you. Pride was your sin and you developed a superiority complex. Looking with contempt at the rest of the world and feeling misunderstood, you became a tyrant and preferred to isolate yourself. There was suffering in this, however, because the people who booed you were the people you wished would admire you.

YOUR GREATEST FEAR is rejection caused by your inability to understand society's codes. Back pain, ear, nose, and throat infections, and a particular sensitivity to cold may be found among carriers of this Moon.

PRIAPUS IN CANCER brings the yin that is indispensable for softening this rock. You are sensitive and know how to care for others, listen to them, and give them tenderness or time, sometimes even helping them meet their material needs. You also act as a welcoming place, a pillar for others, but you must be careful not to do too much for them and let them lead their own lives.

○ BLACK MOON IN AQUARIUS—PRIAPUS IN LEO: MARGINALITY VS SOCIABILITY

Originally, the Black Moon in Aquarius belonged to a humanistic and inspired person. You had a vision of the future and carried out projects for the benefit of everyone else. But this desire to do things eventually made you stand out and feel isolated. You only had the end goal in mind and did not think about the method. You paid no attention to the remarks, reactions, or misunderstanding around you; you were ready to revolutionize the world all by yourself. You eventually arrived on the verge of insanity. This is how your primal fear developed: by becoming a misunderstood visionary, you also became marginalized.

YOUR GREATEST FEAR is driven by a phobia of descending into madness, so you cannot bear to be around people who display even the most minor symptoms. Problems linked to the nervous system are found in the Black Moon in Aquarius.

PRIAPUS IN LEO replaces you at the center of the community. You are confident in your personal radiance and take on projects that are just the right size for you. You are appreciated for your steadfastness and solidarity. People's admiration for you is measured and reassuring. You avoid situations off the beaten path and move within a restrained and manageable framework.

○ BLACK MOON IN PISCES—PRIAPUS IN VIRGO: MADNESS VS MASTERY

The Black Moon in Pisces is searching for mysticism and the sacred. Your need to take care of the world guided your spirituality. You were able to form bridges between worlds because you were channelers or mediums. You used to live in the highest spheres but after spending so much time on these higher planes you lost your grip on reality and your incarnate self.

YOUR GREATEST FEAR is losing your bearings or going insane, and you have a tendency to use substances that trap you inside these irrational worlds. You are devoured by something greater than yourself that you have not successfully mastered.

PRIAPUS IN VIRGO brings you back down to Earth. You value rigor and intellectual analysis. You are present for other people but this time in a material and pragmatic way; you are helpers working in the social or humanitarian spheres and managing logistics and governance. Your simplicity and uprightness attract compliments from those close to you. You are people who can be counted on—the ones who know how to instill order and give advice without seeking glory— and are happy being in your rightful place.

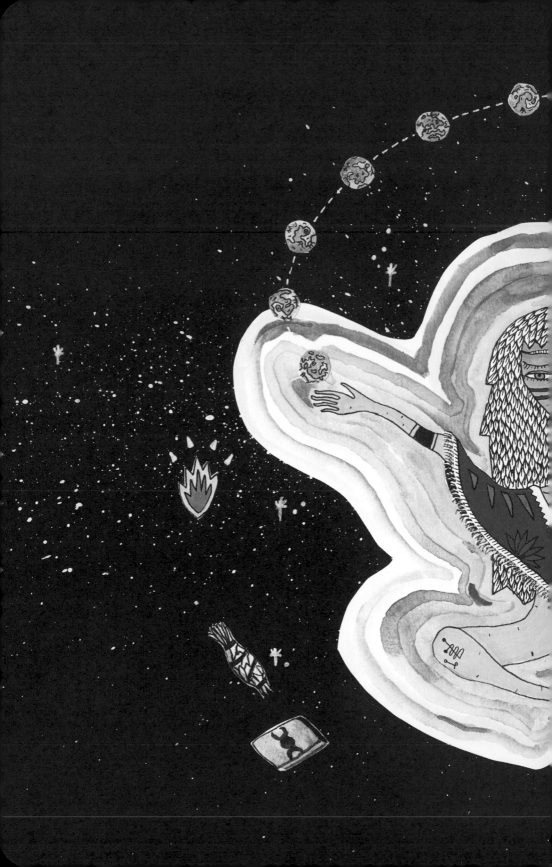

YOUR JOURNEY WITH THE MOON

The Moon is fascinating. She calms and cradles us and at the same time she shakes us up and strips our soul bare. Her cyclical force works in tandem with several other powers: energies, the seasons, plants, and the great female archetypes. Throughout the course of the energetic year, which begins in March, you can learn to work with these alliances by following the New Moon and Full Moon. This will deepen your perceptions of the world and of yourself and this discovery will bring rituals into your life that you can perform during each great lunar portal. Over time this will open the source within you, the source of healing, discovery, questioning, wisdom, and comprehension that will herald the wild woman's great return.

○ THE FULL MOON AND THE NEW MOON

Every month you will perceive the energies linked to the Full Moon and the power, gratitude, dreams, and recharging that characterize this lunar phase. You will do the same during the New Moon phase of purification, new beginnings, and updating intentions. Everything is energy and we cannot go against this rule.

Through meditation and mantras, you can connect lunar energies to your chakras. There are seven chakras and they are located along a channel stretching from the perineum to the top of the head. *Chakra* is a Sanskrit word that means "wheel." These small spinning wheels are portals through which energy passes and are the basis for ayurvedic medicine which, like Chinese medicine, focuses on energetic pathways. The first chakra, Muladhara, is the root chakra in the perineal region. The second, Svhadhishana, the sacral chakra, is located above the pubic bone a few inches below the belly button. The third chakra, Manipura, is at the center of the solar plexus. The fourth, Anahata, is the heart chakra and is located in the center of the chest. Vishuddha, the fifth chakra, belongs to the throat, and the sixth, Ajna, is a point in the middle of the forehead slightly above the eyebrows. This is what is known as the third eye. Last is Sahaswara, the seventh chakra located at the crown of the head. Tending to the energies of these chakras each month allows you to be in harmony with the great lunar influences that are acting in your inner world and relationships.

○ WITCH'S MOON

The "witch's" moon offers us a symbolic decryption of the Full Moon each month that is based on the neopagan traditions of Wicca and shamanism (totemic animals, vegetal animism). You will explore the energies of these "witch" themes, all of which offer an invisible link to a secular spirituality and leave plenty of room for poetry and imagination. Wicca borrows from pagan customs and encourages living in osmosis with nature and the sacred. The movement was born in England under the leadership of Gerald Gardner in the 1950s and later became popular in the United States, particularly in feminist circles. It offers a system of free belief without dogma. Rituals are very present and are performed with respect for Mother Earth. Like shamanism, Wicca opens an unprecedented area of feminine exploration as well as a search for independence and personal power—not so this power can be exerted over others, but so you can lead a powerful and authentic existence.

○ THE EIGHT FESTIVALS OF THE PAGAN YEAR

The Moon was humanity's first temporal marker and the lunar cycles allowed humans to organize themselves into societies. Cosmic time could then be broken down into units for practical use and this formed the basis for pagan ceremonies and agricultural work.

The seasons guide the rhythm of our lives. For pagans there are eight important periods of the year. Each one is associated with a festival and appears in what is called the "Wheel of the Year." This wheel is divided in the following fashion: the summer and winter solstices (Litha and Yule) and the spring and autumn equinoxes (Ostara and Mabon) are Minor or Green Sabbats. Between them are the Major or White Sabbats known as the "festivals of fire." Their names are Samhain, Beltane, Lughnasadh, and Imbolc. These eight festivals marking the passage of each year align with the eight lunar phases that are read in the same cyclical fashion. Yule corresponds with the phase of the New Moon; Imbolc the first

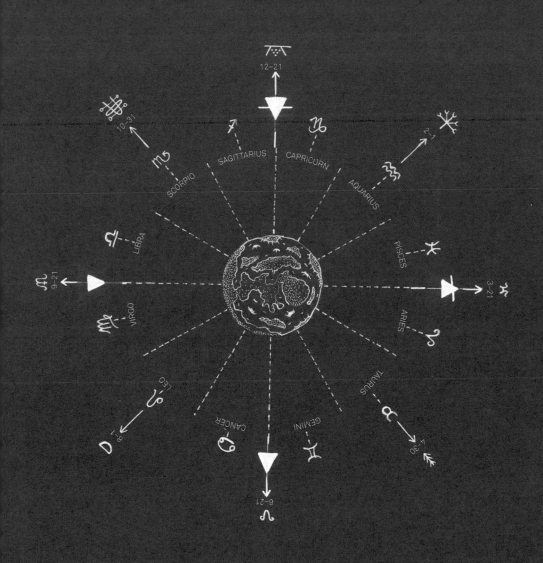

12-21

10-31

2-1

9-21

3-21

6-21

SAGITTARIUS

CAPRICORN

SCORPIO

AQUARIUS

LIBRA

PISCES

VIRGO

ARIES

LEO

TAURUS

CANCER

GEMINI

4-30

YULE   OSTARA   LITHA   MABON

IMBOLC   BELTANE   LUGHNASADH   SAMHAIN

crescent; Ostara the first quarter; Beltane the waxing gibbous; Litha the Full Moon; Lughnasadh the waning gibbous; Mabon the last quarter; and Samhain coincides with the last crescent before the cycle starts again with Yule and the New Moon.

○ PLANT SPIRIT

Throughout this book we will be working with a different plant energy for each month's Moon. Herbs are linked to the cycle of the seasons and have a powerful connection to both nature and human history. Men and women, herbalists and witches, have always given thanks for the power of the plant world and everyone from priestesses to druids and shamans has respected and venerated plants' sacred qualities and used them for their healing potential and high vibrations during rituals.

Simple plant remedies using medicinal and aromatic plants were most often used by women, who were consulted by every layer of society for anything from aches and pains to critical emergencies. Hildegarde of Bingen (1098–1179) is the embodiment of the female herbalist. She was an abbess, a woman of letters, a visionary, a lithotherapist, and a musician. After her story was rediscovered in the late 1970s, she was canonized in 2012. Today her impassioned writings are widely distributed and are helping reintroduce us to plant medicine. As though her death sealed the fate of all women, the end of the twelfth century was a turning point in human history: the first pyres were set alight in Europe and would not be extinguished until six centuries later. This time of persecution shows the extent to which society had encouraged an irrational fear of these women, who were forced to abandon their knowledge of plants or share it with others in secret. As women, reconnecting with this knowledge today lets us take back a little of the power that was denied us years ago. The plants I mention in this book are usually sold by an herbalist. If you choose to pick your own, stick to ones that grow in preserved areas far away from roads, homes, and fields that may be chemically treated. Only pick plants you know well or have them checked by an herbalist or pharmacist. Follow the phases of the Moon and a lunar calendar to harvest leaves, flowers, and roots at the right moment when their energetic charge is at its peak. You should always harvest when the Moon is ascending (something we don't usually take into consideration when gardening). Treat these medicinal herbs with humility and respect. I suggest using them "naturally" either through burning or preparing a tea. Their use should not be taken lightly, and they should not be administered without medical approval, particularly in children, women who are pregnant or breastfeeding, and the elderly. The plants I include should not replace medical treatment.

○ FEMININE ARCHETYPE

The feminine archetypes mentioned on this journey I am offering you come from a variety of different cosmogonies, Ancient Greek and Egyptian mythologies, and Native American, Celtic, African, and South American cultures. These goddesses respond with their own energies to the energies of the months they incarnate. With their universal motifs they become guides that open paths to evolution and transformation. They form the bridge between a common mythology and your individual existence and invite you to use their qualities and powers to nourish your own awakening as you pass through the pivotal stages of your life.

Each moon goddess represents a particular energy, and working with these archetypes will reveal a different facet of your femininity each month. You will discover the parts of you that are creative, intuitive, wise, inspiring, visionary, powerful, combative, maternal, wild, and pioneering. Integrating these goddesses into your rituals will help you develop this connection so you can envision them as familiar forces that will serve as anchors and resources throughout your life. This is the chance to develop your spiritual side as you become part of the boiling cauldron of ancestral beliefs.

○ RITUALS

The ritual is a physical and temporal space that is opened to give symbolic substance to an intention, a need to honor a passage, a personal evolution, a healing, or to reconnect and give thanks. It is a psychomagic act that anchors your intentions in reality and in the present moment and celebrates your spiritual connections. The objects used in your lunar rituals like candles and incense take part in the magic of the moment and help you achieve your goal. These ceremonies do not need to be very complicated and are merely intended to remove you—symbolically—from your day, your thoughts, and your habits so you can enter a sacred space where words and intentions have a deeper meaning and a wider scope.

You can create your own altar by bringing together objects that will give you the anchoring you need for your practices: stones, a shell, flowers, etc. During each ritual you will open your sacred space to prepare yourself to welcome energies with symbols of the four elements. For Water, for example, you can pour spring water into a bowl. For Fire, you can light a candle. For Air you can burn purifiers like incense, sage, palo santo or "sacred wood," and sacred plants. For Earth you can pick up a stone or plant. At the end of each ritual you will close your sacred space by thanking the guides and energies that are present as you blow out the candles.

Performing a lunar ritual during the Full Moon or New Moon teaches you to be in harmony with the energy of these special phases and to reconnect to them. This allows you to solidify your link with the Moon and to plant your thinking in the present. You will then feel that you belong to a greater whole. These rituals are the time to set intentions, ask questions, give thanks, honor, and heal. Each of you will find the path you want to take that resonates with your inner expectations.

Part of what makes rituals such rich experiences is that they can be performed in groups, shared with others, and can always be created or recreated. The best rituals are the ones you feel ownership of: these rituals have a deeper resonance in you and offer a space of freedom and affirmation of your power.

MARCH

REVIVAL

MARCH ○ FULL MOON
REBIRTH

The March Moon can bring about a strong desire for self-affirmation. The time has come to think about new projects, start new activities, and abandon what you no longer want. Reveal your potential and choose to be fully yourself. Set your intentions with faith and intensity and they will bring about your rebirth. Your projects are still in the stage of psychological preparation and intellectual construction, but this is a necessary step that forms the foundation for your future. The Full Moon in March is here to help you make plans for the next nine months of the year: you envision new beginnings, find the means to take action, space out each task, organize your time, and plan. This Moon is the last in the cycle of cold Moons and she opens you to the nascent energy of spring-time, whose forces are rising from the Earth like the sap in the trees. These powerful telluric energies invite you to dive into yourself to illuminate your darkest areas and fill them with light. Step forward without hesitation on this quest for inner truth. Spring, a symbol of renewal and birth, is also the ideal season for taking part in new physical activities and pushing the limits of your body a little further.

You can create and prepare a fertile place by letting yourself be swept up in the energy of the moment. This energy will push you to look outward, leave your comfort zone, and slough off what held you back during the dark winter. Reinforce your anchor, in particular by opening your first chakra, so you can throw yourself wholeheartedly into the ascending movement. You may choose to begin all of this with the famous "spring cleaning" that symbolically marks a new start.

MULADHARA CHAKRA is the root chakra located in the perineum. Meditate with the mantra of the March Full Moon while concentrating on the first chakra. Feel its red light grow brighter and spread through this area of your body.

MANTRA: "I am conscious of my body and its needs. I listen to and respect them."

INTENTIONS: I am entering a new cycle of ascending energy and strength. I am leaving behind the heavy coat of winter to welcome in the fresh light of the present moment.

LUSTRAL WATER RITUAL

You will need a fairly large bowl or other container, water, dandelion flowers, or an essential oil (sandalwood, cedar, lavender, frankincense, sage). **O**pen your sacred space.

Visualize the Moon or look directly at her. Take the time to focus on your breathing and become aware of the sensation each time you inhale and exhale. Place your hands on your heart during these breaths. Connect to Artemis so she can open the path of inner strength to you.

Pour the water into the bowl and add the flowers or essential oil, then wait a few moments and speak your purification intention. For example: "Great Moon, with this water I allow you to purify me."

When you feel ready, place your hands in the water and wash them, stating clearly what you wish to be "cleansed."

When you have finished, give thanks to the Moon and close the sacred space.

MARCH ● NEW MOON
INTUITION

This New Moon is dedicated entirely to the power of your spiritual connections and the blossoming of your intuition. Use this opening to your inner world to set intentions for renewal, remaining attentive to the signs that were sent to you before, during, and after this New Moon. This Moon is particularly suited to meditation in nature. You can recharge yourself in the heart of Mother Earth, letting her song vibrate within you, and in turn become a vehicle for the subtle messages she exudes. Find your fundamental essence by walking barefoot, taking nature baths, and connecting to trees. This is the right moment to practice ecotherapy and use the forces of nature that are beginning to awaken. Rediscover yourself and allow the wild woman to wake up. Her intuition is powerful and she uses all of her senses: like her, you can smell, taste, listen, watch, touch, and sharpen your sensations. This awakening of your third eye takes place through this incarnational relationship with the world, and without it you will not be able to expand your spiritual elevation. If you live in a town or city you can decorate the interior of your living space with plants, whose energies are all beneficial.

AJNA CHAKRA is the third eye and intuition center located in the middle of the forehead between the eyebrows. Meditate with the mantra of the March New Moon, concentrating on the sixth chakra. Feel its indigo light grow brighter and spread throughout this area of your body.
MANTRA: "I open the door for the creative visions living in me and allow them to radiate within me."
INTENTIONS: I will develop my intuition through contact with nature in order to renew my being.

AUTOMATIC WRITING RITUAL
You will need a few bells, chimes, or Tibetan singing bowls, a few sheets of paper, and a pencil.
Open your sacred space by lighting a candle (white for spirituality or green for the Earth element) either at dusk or before sunrise.
Play your instruments and let the air fill with these sounds. Feel your body fill with these vibrations.
Walk barefoot, somewhere in nature if possible, either on grass, dirt, or sand. Connect yourself to the Earth and feel your root chakra opening. Let telluric energy rise along your spinal column to settle at your third eye.
When you want to, take a piece of paper and let your hand write intuitively.
Hold onto these intuitive messages. They reveal your deepest needs. Reread them in a few months to observe your journey.
When you have finished, extinguish the candle and close the sacred space.

CROW ☆ SAP

THE BEGINNING OF THE CYCLE

This Full Moon is the last cold Moon of the season and carries all of the innerness of winter as well as the promise of spring's rebirth: the seeds you have kept safe for several months are now ready to be planted. She is sometimes called the "Sap Moon" because she is in symbiosis with the new season that is arriving.

The March Full Moon is also called the "Crow Moon." In Wicca the crow symbolizes the magic of existence and the cycle of birth and death. Working with this Moon leads you to ask questions about the notion of rebirth in your own life at a time when you are undergoing a profound and significant internal transformation. The crow, linked to the Air element, brings distance and height that allow you to see situations in their entirety, accept the past, and anticipate the future. The Crow Moon leads you down the path to healing and you may need a time of isolation while you confront your fears and courageously cross through areas of darkness to reach awakening. The crow is a protective figure in many cultures and announces the arrival of danger, but can also be a messenger of hope and a traveler carrying light through the darkness.

Beneath the light of the Crow Moon, in your space of contemplation, ask for her protection and ask yourself: How do I want to begin this new cycle? What past strength do I need to move forward and what would I like to leave behind?

MARCH ○ PAGAN FESTIVAL

OSTARA

SPRING EQUINOX SABBAT: MARCH 21

This equinox takes place on March 20th or 21st, depending on the year, and marks the return of light. After the winter season, a time of interiority and being inside, the forces of nature emerge from the depths.

The Earth is reawakened, sap rises in trees and plants, and the songs of birds resound more powerfully than before. This passage of time carries fertility and creativity. Intentions set during the dark retreat of winter take on meaning and shape. By stepping through this energetic portal, you enter the season of spring that your body has been preparing to welcome for several weeks now. The equinox symbolizes awakening and is the epitome of the very season that it ushers in.

The pagan festival of Ostara has always been used to celebrate this time of year and its perfect equilibrium between light and dark, day and night. The masculine yang and feminine yin are also equally powerful at this time. It is a period of harmony symbolized by air and wood and its color is green. Ostara, whose Germanic etymology is a reference to the east, is also linked to the Anglo-Saxon goddess Eostre, later leading to words like "Easter" and "East." The egg, a symbol of birth and life in many cosmogonies, is also associated with this festival. Learning to recognize these energies will help you choose the right time to put the ideas you have formed over the past six months into action.

SEED RITUAL

You will need a sheet of paper, a pen, a potted plant, and some seeds.
Open your sacred space by mindfully connecting to the four elements: Air, Fire, Water, and Earth.
Focus on your breathing. Trace a vertical line down the center of the paper. On the left side, write down what you would like to leave behind using positive affirmations. On the right side, write down what you would like to see grow and blossom, what you would like to develop. Begin each sentence with "I ask for the rebirth of . . ." or "I ask for fertility for . . ."
When you have finished, take a seed for each of your affirmations, place the seeds in the middle of the paper, and fold it. Leave the paper in contact with the Earth (under a pot or buried in the ground in a small bag if you have a yard) until the next Full Moon.
Close the sacred space.
At the next Full Moon, open your sacred space and look at your sheet of paper again. After rereading your affirmations, burn the paper and plant the seeds in the ground. Then close the circle.

DANDELION

NAMES: The dandelion (*Taraxacum officinale*) is also known as the pissabed, lion's tooth, dog-posy, shepherd's clock, golden florin, monk's head, and mole's salad.

IT GROWS wherever it can find a small corner of grass along a road, on the edge of forests, in fields, meadows and yards, marshes, and in cities near cracks in the asphalt.

PROPERTIES: The dandelion helps cleanse the body after it has accumulated toxins during the winter and acts specifically on the liver. Its diuretic properties are evidenced by its "pissabed" common name and it also facilitates digestion. This time of year is perfect for using it in a tincture with other plants like stinging nettle, elderberry, or meadowsweet. It resonates with springtime energies because it supports metabolic awakening and brings balance.

SYMBOLISM: As a spring plant the dandelion embodies the life force because it grows even in harsh conditions. It is linked to the cycle of life (rebirth and death) because its leaves are eaten in the spring and its roots are pulled up at the end of summer. In spring, its flower—a serrated crown with a deep and luminous yellow color worthy of its "lion's tooth" name—represents the Sun. In autumn, its downy and filmy white fruits symbolize the Moon. Its appearance during the latter season resembles a crystal ball and we often call upon its powers of divination spontaneously by blowing on it to see how many years we'll have to wait to get married, how many children we will have, or some other encrypted response. The dandelion is connected to the Air element and used to serve as an offering to the Goddess. It was also used to develop dream capabilities and strengthen powers of clairvoyance.

ARTEMIS

THE FREE AND INDEPENDENT WOMAN

Artemis, the Greek goddess of hunting, is one of the major moon goddesses. Along with Hecate, the darkest of the moon goddesses, and Selene, who represents the Moon in full bloom, she is one of the three faces of the lunar woman. Artemis is linked to the wild world and draws from it its strength and vibrancy. As a virgin goddess she watches over births, young children, and young women in particular. She symbolizes movement, action, freedom, and an untamable spirit that is often associated with the Amazon women, who also used bows and arrows. She is depicted as a young and athletic woman with a crescent moon above her forehead. She is the goddess of initiations. Jungian psychoanalyst Jean Shinoda Bolen describes her as a guide for the sacred feminine who embodies the emergence of the activist woman in feminist thought.

THE WARRIOR GODDESS

Let's not forget that March carries the name of a warrior god. This is why the energies this month require us to reveal our potential as fighting women. Like the young shoots in spring that have to pierce the cold earth to reach for the sky, no goddess but Artemis better personifies this passionate energy, vigor, and thirst for life.

Like Artemis, dare to become this powerful bear-woman: strong-willed, solitary, connected to the Earth and the cycles of nature, and courageous and strong enough to fight against adversity. This goddess is characterized by her need for sisterhood and her concern for equality in relationships with men. Artemis and Apollo, her twin brother, represent two faces of the same coin: the Moon on one side and the Sun on the other. You carry these two energies within you and can use them to become a woman who is both a conqueror and a sensitive being.

Form an alliance with Artemis by invoking her during your rituals and meditations. She will be able to guide your impulses and balance your masculine and feminine energies. You will, thanks to her, awaken the ancestral wisdom that is buried within you, strengthen your will, and cultivate your independence.

APRIL

FERTILITY

INTENSITY

This Moon is also called the "Pink Moon" and is the first Full Moon after Easter. Her influence extends from the last New Moon to the next, covering an entire cycle. She is powerful and extremely active and has a strong impact on all of us. You will have to adapt to these external vibrations of greater and greater intensity.

On the night of this Full Moon we open ourselves to the masculine period of the year. We activate our power of action while regulating our simmering impulses. Be a volcano that groans in its depths and allow your tears to fall if the pressure is too great; they are the water that tempers this creative flame. Learn to calm yourself to avoid overexertion. Allow your body to use these complementary energies to unfurl your sexuality and augment your creativity. Your sacred chakra plays a significant role; use the forces at work and allow yourself to be carried by the animal power that is connected to your truest self.

Projects that are in phase with your deepest desires will begin to emerge around this Moon, and what you asked for during the dark wintertime can now be set in motion. You are part of an exciting cycle in which you can fertilize your internal soil and sow the seeds of change that will have a long-term impact on your life. This Moon also carries within her a violence that may lead your projects to destruction as much as success. Remain vigilant and know how to dedicate yourself to a project without skipping important steps. If you don't do this you risk seeing your initiatives go up in smoke.

SVADHISTHANA CHAKRA is the sacral chakra located a few inches below the belly button, just above the genital organs. Meditate with the mantra of the April Full Moon while concentrating on your second chakra. Feel its orange light grow brighter and spread throughout this area of your body.

MANTRA: "I listen to, accept, and respect my desire."

INTENTIONS: I honor myself by taking care of my body and soul. I absorb yang energies by revealing my creativity and sexuality.

CREATIVE FERTILITY RITUAL

You will need a candle, a leaf, colored pencils, paint, and markers.

Open the circle. Light a candle with the intention to honor Cybele, goddess of trance, and the all-powerful Mother Earth.

Begin by settling the physical body, here and now, and become aware of how you are sitting. Take a few mindful deep breaths. Tonight, the round and radiant Moon will descend into you.

Imagine that a trap door is opening at the crown of your head. A golden thread descends vertically from the Moon, enters through this opening, and goes all the way down to your uterus. Once there, it gently blows a golden powder into you. Your uterus fills with light.

Place your hands on your stomach and feel the beneficial warmth.

When you feel full, allow the thread to go back up and hold onto this powerful creative energy.

Take your leaf, paintbrushes, pens, pencils, and your nondominant hand and begin working on an intuitive creation. Appreciate the pleasure of creating without limits.

Give thanks to the Moon and Cybele. Close the circle.

APRIL ● NEW MOON
ACTION

This New Moon opens wide the doors to your personal fulfillment. You are in the heart of your life path. Think with sincerity about the best direction to take for your evolution and use an awareness of your recent experiences to remind yourself of the lessons they taught you. The New Moon's ascending energies literally push you toward your rebirth. You are in a portal with tonalities that may be bothersome, violent, or a source of tension when everything seems to be telling you that you are ready. Ready to claim your freedom like the phoenix, consuming what no longer exists and rising up from the ashes of what was. This New Moon pushes you to act more and think less. Your actions during this period reveal what is truly important to you. Rejoice to have this opportunity to become the creator of your own existence. Absorb the vibrations rising up from the bowels of Mother Earth. When you are anchored in your first chakra you have the potential to transform these vibrations to nourish your individual actions. Be thankful that you are in exactly the right place when you align yourself with the energetic repercussions of this New Moon, choose to stop living in darkness, and finally step into the light. Your body, carried by the Earth, is ready to give love and show affection. This is a moment of physical sharing both with nature and with those dear to us.

MULADHARA CHAKRA is the root chakra located in the perineum. Meditate with the mantra of the April Full Moon while concentrating on the first chakra. Feel its red light grow brighter and spread throughout this area of your body.

MANTRA: "I am the Earth. She carries me, I carry her."

INTENTIONS: Filled with high energies, I am growing into a new me; not quite different, but no longer quite the same.

RITUAL FOR UNITING EARTH AND MOON ENERGIES

Choose music with percussion or use a percussion instrument. Gather what you need to make a real or symbolic fire (a candle, for example). Remove your shoes and socks.

Open the circle. Light a fire if you are outside or a candle if you are inside. Invoke Cybele, goddess of trance, who connects us and makes the Earth vibrate with her music. Ask her to put you in direct contact with your instinct and the wild part of you that she symbolizes.

Place your hands on your uterus with the intention to connect to the Moon. Take a few minutes to savor these sensations. In rhythm to the music, gently allow yourself to be guided by these lunar energies in an intuitive dance. Move in vibration without intention or reflection. Let go of your thoughts and return to the vibration, dancing without worrying about what is happening around you. Take pleasure in the freedom that this lunar dance procures for you.

Give thanks to the Earth and Cybele. Close the circle.

APRIL ○ WITCH'S MOON

SEED ☆ FISH

THE STIRRINGS OF FERTILITY

In April we celebrate the Moon of seeds and fish who breathes a surge of fertility into the Earth. She is connected to seeds because this is the time when seeds are planted in our gardens. Native Americans call her the "Fish Moon" because the fish symbolizes fertility and abundance and echoes the prosperous energies of this month. Known for fertility and wisdom, she marks the beginning of a cycle and brings significant changes that will ask you about your ability to transform yourself. This Moon of beginnings encourages you to leap into action. She has a bond with the east, where the Sun rises, and Water, the element of fish, and possesses tremendous powers of regeneration. Many dreams of fertility will appear under this Moon of transition and invite you to explore your psyche. Allow yourself to be inhabited and welcome the energies descending from the Moon as well as those rising from the Earth into your verticality. Under the auspices of the Fish Moon you open yourself to all of the possibilities at the start of this season. Ask yourself about your capacity for self-renewal. What deep desire would you like to kindle? What feeling do you want to send out to honor your creative power?

APRIL ○ PAGAN FESTIVAL

BELTANE

APRIL 30

Beltane is celebrated halfway between the spring equinox and summer solstice and is an important Sabbat festival as well as the last celebration of the dark season. It is called "Witches' Night" because it is linked to the esoteric world and sometimes "Walpurgis Night" because this pagan festival marking the passing of spring—which had spread throughout Europe—was strongly condemned by Christian leaders who replaced it with a celebration of Saint Walpurgis on the same day. This festival of fire has marked the end of winter ever since Antiquity and helps us emerge from our innerness and free ourselves of our dark parts.

On the Wheel of the Year, Beltane is one of two festivals that involve an extensive use of magic: Samhain opens the dark season and Beltane closes it. These are times of great spiritual connection, two portals during which the worlds open halfway. The Buddhist festival of Wesak is celebrated at this same time of the year around the world. It is a blessing of universal love that unites pagan, Christlike, and Buddhist energies and offers healing and spiritual transmutation.

As the pagan celebration of fertility, Beltane embodies the love connected to the forces of nature, the awakening of the senses, and the call to unite your body with others in its sacred dimension. On the night of the festival, men and women would traditionally put up a decorated pole or plant a May Tree, a symbol of the renewal of springtime forces, and organize joyous and sensual fire dances. In Wicca, this is the night when the horned god, a masculine figure of our primitive nature, impregnates the Goddess. Be aware that your sexual energy is creative and harmonize with the masculine and feminine polarities that you carry within you. Celebrate the forces present on this night and reconnect with your desire. Reclaim your sexuality and glorify the creative power of your womb.

RITUAL FOR DRAWING ENERGY UP FROM THE EARTH

You will need a bowl, dried meadowsweet flowers, and filtered or spring water.

Open the circle.

Fill the bowl with water and place the meadowsweet flowers in the water. This plant is used during rites of passage and initiations because it strengthens the potential for transformation and facilitates the ascension of your consciousness. Let the flowers infuse for a few minutes.

Take a deep breath in to center your energy and a long breath out to anchor your body to the earth. With the intention to purify yourself, drink a sip of the water then use it to wash your hands, forearms, and feet.

Stand and focus on a point on the ground. Begin to sing and dance, turning around this point. The rotation of your dance will lead to a rising of energy from the ground.

When you begin to feel this energy, stop the dance, lift your arms, and clasp your hands together in a point above your head. Let the energy rise all the way up and spread around you through the tips of your fingers. Close the circle.

APRIL ○ PLANT SPIRIT
MEADOWSWEET

NAMES: Meadowsweet (*Spiraea ulmaria*) is also known as goatsbeard, pride of the meadow, queen of the meadow, bridewort, or dolloff.

IT GROWS in humid areas near lakes, rivers, streams, and marshes. It is found in Europe and Asia. It blooms from June to September but the best time to harvest it is Saint John's Eve in June when its energies are most powerful and its therapeutic properties are most effective. With its delicately honeyed scent it perfumes the days of summer, honoring change and celebrating the renewal of the season.

PROPERTIES: Meadowsweet is a very effective anti-inflammatory and soothes joint and rheumatic pain. It also has detoxifying, diuretic, and analgesic effects and contains derivatives of salicylic acid, the active ingredient in aspirin. All of its parts (flowers, leaves, and roots) can be consumed and it has also been used since the Neolithic period to flavor drinks.

SYMBOLISM: Meadowsweet is a sacred plant and is one of the great pillars of traditional druidic herbalism along with water mint and vervain. During rites of passage and initiations, meadowsweet was one of the offerings placed at burial sites and necropolises. It symbolizes the phases of evolution and was often brought to newlyweds to mark their union and perfume their clothing and ceremony with its subtle honey scent. It is linked to Air, the element of spring, and also to Water, because it grows in honor of the water god in damp areas.

APRIL ○ FEMININE ARCHETYPE
CYBELE
THE INSTINCTIVE WOMAN

Cybele is a mother goddess who embodies the wildest parts of nature and is the all-powerful goddess archetype. The cult of Cybele originated in the Middle East and eventually reached Greece and Rome, where her aura of power and violence remains intact. She was raised by lions and is often depicted in their company. A number of mysterious and violent cults were captivated by her and made her the exclusive object of their worship. Ritual celebrations for Cybele were often marked with bull's blood that was used to baptize her disciples. In the spring, these cults held castration ceremonies for young men because only eunuchs had the right to serve her. She had been born a hermaphrodite from the seed of Zeus and the gods decided to remove her masculine part by castrating her, forcing her to be reborn as a woman. The violence that characterized her cult has its roots in this story.

THE WILD GODDESS
Cybele is the guardian of the wild world, primitive nature, and animals and plants, and is the goddess of mountains and pine trees, symbols of transcendence. She holds the key that opens the doors to the subterranean world. Also linked to music, she bequeathed to humans the art of dance and the instruments whose sounds shake the depths of the Earth and resonate to liberate their souls. Honor Cybele in the lavish month of April while nature unfurls itself by getting in touch with your instinct and animality, which only desire to be reunited with the highly civilized woman you show the world. Let your hair down, take off your clothes, take up your cymbals, and smell the earth, cry out to the Moon, and drink from the flowing river. Cybele the mother goddess offers nature to you on a silver platter. Call her into your rituals and meditations and ask her to offer you the key to the great All. This is something that is much bigger than you but is also something you carry in your sacred belly, the cradle of fertility.

MAY

HARMONY

MAY ○ FULL MOON
AUTHENTICITY

The night of this Full Moon marks a special moment in your personal journey. The Moon asks you about your attachment to the values at the core of your personality, your ethics, and your integrity. How can you continue to walk along this path if you are not fully living out your verticality? You evolve, you try different things, but are you always in phase with your authenticity in your life and relationships? What story are you telling yourself? What screen have you put up to avoid confronting a situation that doesn't work for you or ending a relationship that is no longer what you want? What are you hiding behind that keeps your true face behind a veil so you can bear your pain in silence? You need to be aware of your actions and their consequences. You must banish fear and lies from your life and offer yourself the chance to stand naked in front of yourself. You are beautiful in your original nudity and have the power to nourish what deserves to be nourished. In the center of your chest, in the solar plexus, you can find this truth and cultivate an attachment to your convictions and beliefs. Using the law of attraction, you can set positive intentions for yourself and remember that what you resist persists. Too much worry paralyzes you. Feed your strength instead of your anxiety. You must stand tall in the dark night and the Moon will show you the radiant path that is open to you.

MANIPURA CHAKRA is the center of the solar plexus. Meditate with the mantra of the May Full Moon while concentrating on the third chakra. Feel its golden light grow brighter and spread throughout this area of your body.
MANTRA: "I anchor myself inside to open myself to others."
INTENTIONS: I seek truth and inner peace. I am aware of my actions and nourish my positive values.

WORD STONES RITUAL
You will need a few flat stones from your nature walks and a white paint marker.
Open the circle.

Place your hands in the center of your chest and connect to the goddess Chang'e, who lives on the Moon. She will allow you to connect to your deep "me" and the consequences of your choices.

Ask her to let you be reborn tonight in greater alignment. Ask her to give you the information you need.

Let the words come to you that are essential right in this moment: anchoring, simplicity, communication, liberty, confidence, intuition, breath, meditation, etc. Write these words on the stones and keep them as divination tools. When you feel lost, they will be able to reconnect you to your deepest needs. If you wish, you can draw or doodle symbols on the stones instead of words.

Close the circle.

MAY ● NEW MOON
PACT

On this dark night, you will make a pact with the Moon. With her help, you will learn how to see yourself in a new way and how to experience profound self-love. Look at yourself honestly and cradle with compassion the parts of your soul that hurt you or that you dislike. You will have to make yourself vulnerable in order to bring love into these dark zones. To do this, continue down this spiritual path and never abandon the way of elevation and ethics. Open your heart. As you learn to love every part of yourself, you will offer others the possibility to do the same for themselves, loving bonds will deepen, and new encounters will happen. At the same time, you will free yourself from toxic relationships of the past, repetitive life schemas, and negative thought patterns. Choose the path of renewal. All of this invisible work requires a great deal of energy, and this great cleansing may take a toll on you. Physical problems may appear. You must be ready for them because these pains have words to pass on. Your body is talking to you about your story, so listen to what it is saying.

ANAHATA CHAKRA is the heart chakra located in the center of the chest. Meditate with the mantra of the May New Moon, concentrating on the fourth chakra. Feel its green light grow brighter and spread throughout this area of your body.

MANTRA: "I feel my being radiating with love for myself and those I love."

INTENTIONS: I am consciously making a pact to love myself.

MOON STICK RITUAL

You will need paint, wool, cotton thread, chimes, gold thread, palo santo sticks, and a few treasures picked up in nature: sticks (hawthorn wood if possible), feathers, shells, etc.

Open the circle.

Ask the New Moon to liberate your inner space to let your creativity thrive.

Burn the sacred wood, palo santo, to purify yourself and connect, then pass your sticks through the smoke to charge them with positive energy.

Allow yourself to express your power through the creation of these power sticks: paint them, tie braided threads around them, and add shells, feathers, and bells with the intention that they will protect you and bring you connection, luck, and strength. Follow your intuition.

Close the circle.

On the next Full Moon, you can recharge your sticks beneath her light.

MAY ○ WITCH'S MOON
FLOWER ☆ HARE
THE BLOSSOMING MOON

This very positive pagan Moon gives you back your energy. Nature is in full bloom and the cycle of summer is beginning. For Native Americans this period culminates in the blossoming of flowers. For you it is the time to observe your progress and realize that the buds have opened and the flowers are showering you with their perfumes and colors. Nature is accompanying your personal evolution and demonstrating its stunning beauty. Under the sweet auspices of this Moon you can begin harvesting medicinal plants; those that are harvested tonight will be charged with the power of moonlight. This Witch's Moon is connected to your fertility and intuition and brings you a unique exhilaration.

The hare, which is a member of the lunar bestiary in many cosmogonies, embodies prosperity and abundance. It symbolizes equilibrium between the worlds and helps you learn to listen. It is a silent animal with large ears, embodying the ability to receive internal messages and integrate your sixth sense in daily life. Under this Flower and Hare Moon, take the time to contemplate nature in all of its expansiveness and profusion. Smell the perfume of the Flower Moon as it sweetens the air and transports you. May you know how to take advantage of Mother Earth's generosity. Ask her to exude into and inspire you. Your body and soul ask only to blossom, and you can help them by summoning this Moon's forces of love. Look at life through the most gentle and serene filter you can. You will become the wild grass that waves beneath the moonlight.

HAWTHORN

NAMES: Hawthorn (*Crataegus laevigata*) is also known as the mayflower, white thorn, and thorn apple.

IT GROWS in hedges and outside forests and woods throughout Europe. It blooms from May to June and its flowers can be harvested while still in the bud.

PROPERTIES: Hawthorn, directly linked to your heart and its chakra, can regulate palpitations, anxiety, and hypertension, and also reinforces cardiac tonicity. It can also be used for sleep problems, anxiety, and feelings of vertigo.

SYMBOLISM: Hawthorn's Latin name comes from the Greek word *kratos* meaning "solid," and this is a tree that you can count on for protection. Shepherds used staffs made out of hawthorn wood to hook the necks of animals in their herd, and families would often place some in the cradle with their young children.

In Ancient Greece this plant symbolized marital bliss, chastity, and fertility. Young newlyweds wore crowns made of hawthorn flowers to bring happiness to their union. It was also often on altars during the wedding ceremony.

In the New Testament the hawthorn tree is associated with the Virgin Mary, who seeks protection under its branches on a stormy night and dries the clothing of the baby Jesus on it. During the Passion, the crown on Christ's head is also made of hawthorn.

This is a magic plant connected to the Fire and Air elements. It is also the tree of fairies and the guardian of sacred places. It is often associated with the festival of Beltane because its flowers are picked on May 1st when their properties are most powerful. Hawthorn repels negative forces but can seal the fate of any person who picks its flowers without making an offering.

CHANG'E

THE WOMAN WHO IS MINDFUL OF HER ACTIONS

Chang'e is one of the most appreciated figures in Chinese culture. She is a moon goddess and elicits a powerful devotion even today. In Taoist spirituality she is the incarnation of the feminine principle, the absolute yin. There are several versions of the myth of Chang'e but they all involve immortality and the Moon she is synonymous with. Chang'e is separated from humans but still watches over them. Her story begins when her husband Hou Yi, a celestial archer, saves the Earth from being set afire by the ten suns. As a reward he is offered an immortality potion that Chang'e discovers and drinks immediately without knowing what it contains. The more of this magic drink she swallows, the higher she soars toward the heavens until she finds herself on the Moon. She chooses to stay and discovers a jade hare who is also an herbalist and together they make medicinal potions. In some versions Chang'e drinks the immortality potion on purpose and is banished to the Moon. In others, one of Hou Yi's disciples tries to steal it from her and Chang'e has no other choice but to drink it and flee to the Moon.

THE GODDESS OF SELF-AWARENESS

Chang'e learned a lesson from her adventure. She had to leave everything behind to pay the price for her transgression and now she knows that every action taken in life can have significant repercussions. With her story in mind, be aware of your actions. Ask yourself what the consequences of your decisions might be. Chang'e does not die; she is reborn somewhere else and as something different, now a part of the endless lunar cycle. Like this goddess you are capable of being reborn. Harmonize your lives in awareness, anchor yourself to the present moment, and keep your feet on the ground. Sometimes it is easier not to confront reality, to go to the Moon instead of facing what you need to in your life. Dare to be who you are. Stop trying to evade and instead have confidence because the answers are within you. Out of this profound internal truth will come harmony and balance. Become the complete woman who is capable of knowing and transforming herself.

JUNE

EXTERNALIZATION

POWER

This Full Moon filled with sap, life, blood, and strength is asking about your power and personal energy. Are you comfortable with it? Can you accept it? Don't hesitate any longer. Throw yourself down this light-filled path because it leads you back to your power. Every single one of us can reclaim it; we simply have to take a stand.

   Look at the color of your soul right here and right now: What are the shackles preventing you from accessing your absolute personal expression? You are called to understand what keeps you from lifting these barriers. The energies of this experience are intense and you will have to tackle them head-on. Find the door to open inside of you and recenter your strength in the second chakra, which is the sexuality center and a portal to the awakening of the kundalini. Call upon your masculine part to free the energies that have accumulated within you and, for some reason, remain blocked. Only a balance of forces can bring the opening needed for the full expression of your feminine power: yin is nothing without her complementary yang. Turn your eyes to the future, free yourself from the past, balance your polarities, and find your wild soul again. These upheavals will be accompanied by a torrent of emotions and an intense connection to the invisible world. Wait to receive signs and messages to guide you along this path and listen to your dreams during this Moon's days of influence. Write them down because they will be precious allies in the months to come.

SVADHISTHANA CHAKRA is a sacral chakra situated a few inches below the navel in the zone above the genital organs. Meditate with the mantra of the June Full Moon while concentrating on your second chakra. Feel its orange light grow brighter and spread throughout this area of your body.

MANTRA: "My creative force is within me; its energy is circulating in every one of my cells."

INTENTIONS: I liberate the powerful woman inside me.

PROPHETESS RITUAL

Prepare a mugwort tea to promote divination and clairvoyance and drink it before beginning the ritual. You will need a candle and a knife.

Open the circle.

Enter into meditation while in a comfortable seated position. Focus your attention on your breath and slowly calm its rhythm.

Let the night adorned with moonlight enfold your body. Feel the way this sheet wraps itself around your hips. The Moon gently cradles you, your whole lower abdomen undulates, and waves of energy flow into your genitals. Feel the heat and energy rising in you.

Now open your soul and ask the Full Moon to send you her visions. You are ready to receive them. Let the symbols come and engrave them on the candle using the knife. You can light this candle each lunar month.

Close the circle.

JUNE ● NEW MOON
EXCHANGE

Under the darkness of this New Moon, as the sparkling veil of truth is lifting, celebrate the authenticity of your relationships. Let energies come up and express themselves in words. Without using a filter, discover your new voice, one that will communicate sincerely with those near and dear to you. It is like a stream inviting you to follow it. It summons the souls who are most important to you and reinforces your desire to unite with the Other. Words weave a bond, and words form a sacred alliance. Seal and affirm the most important relationships in your lives under this New Moon. This is a perfect night for making your love song heard and celebrating sharing with others. A great deal of subtle information circulates in the month of June, and you may pick up on messages that reinforce your personal development because you are in a period of ascension and self-affirmation. Your need for exchange is intense: take your turn to speak and give voice to your truth. But be careful not to overextend yourself. Recenter yourself in your uterine area. This is your compass and anchoring point. Set aside your thoughts and return to yourself, going down into your belly where your truth is found. Listen to it and let it spring up and rise to your throat chakra, the chakra of speaking. Allow the right words to be spoken, and what must be said will now be out in the open.

VISHUDDA CHAKRA is the throat chakra. Meditate with the mantra of the June New Moon while concentrating on the fifth chakra. Feel its blue light grow brighter and spread throughout this area of your body.

MANTRA: "My thoughts are clear and my words are impeccable."

INTENTIONS: My words are the mirrors of my soul. Pointing them toward the people I love nourishes my relationships and elevates me.

MUGWORT OIL RITUAL

You will need a sterilized jar or other container, gauze, string, vegetable oil, and dried mugwort. This technique goes back to Antiquity when plant oils were used for massages, therapeutic treatments, and culinary preparations.

Open the circle and call upon the Great Goddess, mother of all mothers, so she can bless your plants.

Fill your jar with dried mugwort, cover with vegetable oil, then cover the jar using the gauze and string so the mixture can breathe.

Let the oil sit in a dark place and stir it regularly.

Close the circle.

After six weeks, strain the mixture and dry the plants. Pour the oil into a sterile flask. This mugwort oil can be used to ease pain, relax your lower belly before menstruation, and release muscle tension. Apply it to your wrists or thymus area if you are feeling low.

JUNE ○ WITCH'S MOON
LOVER ☆ HONEY
THE SHARING OF LOVE

In the pagan tradition, seeing the Full Moon rise in June is synonymous with rejoicing. All the names given to this Full Moon evoke gentleness, pleasure, and union. This is the time to create or strengthen bonds of love. Summer is beginning and your body is externalizing its need for physical experience. Your skin is the vector for your emotions.

This Moon symbolizes marriage, and honey is the offering. In some countries wedding bands were dipped in honey to bring happiness to newlyweds and kindle their desire for one another. Honey evokes sweetness and the pleasure of the senses. Also called the "Strawberry Moon," this Moon is linked to this time of harvest and abundance and the temptation that this fruit has represented since the Middle Ages. In Nordic mythology the strawberry is associated with Freya, a mother goddess who gives humans pleasure, reward, and shared experiences. This Moon is a moment of physical ecstasy and strong emotions. Her energies are connected to earthly energies and bring about an elevation of consciousness, strengthened spirituality, and a dancing of the body and soul.

Under the nurturing rays of the Moon, breathe, brush, touch, taste, and dare to enjoy what nature is offering so generously. Celebrate this explosion of the senses. Externalize your feelings and discover the simple pleasure of being one with Mother Earth. Everything becomes possible if you do it with heart and authenticity.

JUNE ○ PAGAN FESTIVAL
LITHA
SUMMER SOLSTICE: JUNE 21

Join in Mother Earth's effervescence by connecting to the magnificent and powerful summer solstice. This fire festival is ancient and we have an instinctive need to celebrate light on the longest day of the year. This is how Nature demonstrates its power at the peak of its energy and abundance. This evening should be shared with those you love, in vibration to the rhythm of vital energy. If you cannot dance around a joyful fire like your ancestors did, create a festive glow in your home by sharing a good meal made with fresh produce and herbs. Sing, take out your instruments, and let your voices fill the air. Dance, buy yourself beautiful flowers, light candles, and celebrate the pleasure of living fully in the present moment. By communing with the energies of the season in this way you are ensuring balance for yourself and using this time to activate protection and healing.

INSTINCTIVE DANCE RITUAL

Accompany your dance with a drum, if you have one, or any music you enjoy that is able to transport you. This ritual will be more intense around a fire in the midst of nature.

Open the circle.

Play an instrument or turn on the music.

Stand barefoot. Breathe and with each inhalation feel a red light penetrating through the arch of your foot and rising through you, flowing through your body. Feel the same light, now a golden color, leaving your nostrils each time you exhale.

After several breaths, let yourself be invaded by the vibrations of the music, moving your feet, legs, hips, stomach, chest, arms, and head.

Liberate your body and sing. During this dance, imagine the red and gold light mixing within you, around you, and with the colors of the people beside you.

When you have finished, close the circle.

JUNE ○ PLANT SPIRIT
MUGWORT

NAMES: Mugwort (*Artemisia vulgaris*) is also known as the felon herb, common wormwood, and chrysanthemum weed. It is part of the group of St. John's healing herbs.

IT GROWS in Europe and around the Mediterranean basin. It is common and often found along trails and in abandoned fields or uncultivated areas. It blooms from late June to October and should be harvested at the beginning of the season, in particular during the summer solstice.

PROPERTIES: Mugwort is an emmenagogue and can relieve menstruation problems and help regulate your cycle. It was commonly used by midwives to make labor easier and ease pain. It can also be used to combat fever, detoxify the liver, or as an antiseptic. It is similar to absinthe— without the same level of toxicity—and has antispasmodic and anti-inflammatory properties.

SYMBOLISM: Mugwort's Latin name is *Artemisia* and it has been associated with the moon goddess Artemis since Ancient Greece. A so-called "sacred feminine" plant, it was frequently used during summer solstice rituals. Belts were made for women to wear while they danced around the fire so the energetic effects of the freshly harvested plant would protect their genital sphere from disease, bring balance to it, and strengthen it. Mugwort is a protective plant and was also hung in wreaths above a home's front door. It was said to have the power to keep venomous animals at bay and coming across it during a walk was a sign of good luck. Mugwort belongs to magical herbalism and is used in white magic for enchantments to chase away evil spirits and black magic spells. It is an herb of power associated with the Earth, Air, and Fire elements and is also the plant of Isis, making it particularly useful for divination; drinking mugwort tea before a seance can amplify clairvoyance. Divination tools can be consecrated by passing them through burning mugwort smoke, and this plant can also be used to call upon allies and guides during rituals. Putting mugwort under your pillow will allow you to have prophetic dreams.

JUNE ○ FEMININE ARCHETYPE
THE MOTHER GODDESS
THE ORIGINAL WOMAN

The Great Goddess is the one who came before all others. Long considered to be a minor figure in ancestral European cults, we have learned through the work of archeologist Marija Gimbutas that she was the cosmogonic representation of woman as the origin of the world and the incarnation of the life cycle because of her ability to unceasingly regenerate and renew herself. People first began worshipping her during the Neolithic period, and archaeomythology has shown the existence of a matriarchal religion that was widespread throughout Europe and lasted until 300–400 BC. Her influence decreased with the simultaneous arrival of writing and the Indo-European invasions. These invaders—who imposed their pantheon and masculine gods on the people they conquered—disrupted the matrilineal order of agrarian European societies. The presence of the Great Goddess cult was not an indication that the social order at the time was matriarchal, but is evidence of a balance between feminine and masculine powers: at the head of these "gylanic" preinvasion communities were queens, clan chieftesses, and priestesses.

The Mother Goddess is associated with lunar themes and motifs and represents regeneration. She embodies the cycle of life, death, and rebirth, and is depicted with maternal and sexual attributes, abundant breasts and buttocks, and symbols of fertility, magic, and procreation. These features can be seen in the Paleolithic Venuses from Laussel, Lespugue, and Willendorf. The Mother Goddess is associated with animals like the ram, bear, deer, and the Water element, a source of life. We also find her disguised as a bird goddess with a beak, wings, breasts, and sometimes the eyes of a nocturnal bird of prey. "V" and "M" symbols were initially thought to be decorative motifs but they are actually a reference to the woman: V is the depiction of the vulva, and M represents the fertile water linked to sexuality and maternity. The widespread images of a serpent goddess are another representation of this Great Goddess.

THE GODDESS OF RADIANT FEMININITY

There is something deeply moving about connecting to the power of this Mother Goddess because she carries in her the origin of humanity and the essence of femininity.

During this month of externalization and self-searching, reunite with your ability to regenerate yourself and create, feeling your uterus vibrating with the evocation of this ancient cult that is an ode to the power of all women. When you pray to her you are creating bridges between the cycles of nature and your own, between telluric and cosmic energies. By entrusting her with your intentions you are in fact addressing the entire universe. Transcend time and space and, like the first women on the floor of their cave, paint your faces red, the color of blood, as a sign of solidarity. Walk beside this ancestral figure of the sacred feminine and be proud to be the new representatives of this divine and wild lineage. Daughters of the Great Goddess, we are all powerful women.

JULY

HEART OPENING

EXALTATION

The Full Moon that follows the summer solstice is filled with the fire energies of the season and brings about powerful internal and external movements. Many things are in motion during this time. In this humming swarm of messages, you must show discernment and find the thread of your inner voice. Your body can become your compass when necessary, so listen to it and decipher its nonverbal language. It is hyperconnected to your five senses and in tune with nature and your environment. It will guide you. Take the time to discover the rhythm of your own heartbeat and feel the blood circulating in your veins. Listen to your pain because it has a message for you. Spiritual energies are expanding and vibrating at your fourth chakra. Welcome them with your heart. This is the moment to walk alongside your guides and allies and ask them to bind your wounds and chase away any fears that are stirred up by this energetic flow. This Full Moon is very destabilizing on an emotional level and can be both thrilling and exhausting.

ANAHATA CHAKRA is the heart chakra located in the center of the chest. Meditate with the mantra of the June Full Moon while concentrating on the fourth chakra. Feel its green light grow brighter and spread throughout this area of your body.

MANTRA: "My heart is a drum whose beating sets the rhythm for my life."

INTENTIONS: I use the energies I have access to with exaltation; I open my heart to receive these messages.

LUNAR BATH RITUAL

Perform this ancestral practice outside. Bring along a bouquet of yarrow for its prophetic powers.

Open the circle in the place you intend to take your lunar bath.

If possible, lie down on the ground. Place the yarrow bouquet on your stomach.

Let your breath descend into your body. With each exhale, feel it settle deeper and deeper into the Earth.

Feel the caress of the moonlight on your skin. Infuse yourself with her energy and feel it enter you each time you inhale.

Open yourself to the prophetic messages and signs you will capture in this meditative state.

When you feel "recharged," give thanks to Grandmother Moon and close the circle.

JULY ● NEW MOON
ELEVATION

This New Moon asks you to examine your place in the world and reveals your karmic lessons: What are you meant to work on in this life? Impressions, sensations, and synchronicities that you weren't aware of before start to appear like missing puzzle pieces. To find the path that leads to your truth, navigate outside your comfort zone. As you welcome these energies you experience a feeling of elevation. This is the time to grow, pass into a new stage of knowledge, evolve spiritually, become confident, and develop a clear awareness. Open your fifth chakra and put words to the messages that are here to shake you up. Know how to use your words to retranscribe what emerges from the depths of your earth-belly. Become fully present in all aspects of your existence. This phase of revelation is sometimes uncomfortable, and the self-knowledge that the New Moon gives you access to is unbelievably intense and can be profoundly unsettling.

VISHUDDHA CHAKRA is the throat chakra. Meditate with the mantra of the July New Moon while concentrating on the fifth chakra. Feel its blue light grow brighter and spread throughout this area of your body.

MANTRA: "I open myself to inner messages and allow them to take flight."

INTENTIONS: I connect myself to all aspects of my being and to the world around me.

SPIRAL WRITING RITUAL

You will need a sheet of paper, a pen, and a few colored pencils.

Open the circle.

When night falls, find a comfortable seat beneath the Moon in a calm place where you will be able to write.

Call upon the goddess Mawu while placing your hands on your uterus. Ask her to open you to every dimension and to help you find your place in the world.

Take a deep breath. Imagine a silver thread traveling up your spine from your uterus and emerging from the crown of your head, stretching all the way to the Moon. Ask her the questions that come to you.

When you feel connected, close your eyes and begin to draw a counter-clockwise spiral, continuing for as long as you want.

When you perceive a message (an emotion, sensation, idea, image, or shape) turn over the sheet of paper and write or draw the symbols, sigils (drawings that enclose a magical intention), signs, words, or images that present themselves to you. Let them guide you.

Give thanks to the Moon for this gift and close the circle.

JULY ○ WITCH'S MOON
THUNDER ☆ BARLEY
NATURE'S POWER

This Moon rises when nature is in a paroxysm of expansion. Scents and colors are exploding, flowers and fruits are ripe, and your senses are sharpened to take advantage of these enticements. You spend most of your time outside, enjoying the long days and gentle nights and taking time to contemplate the sky. Barley is connected to the first harvests and is known for its resistant nature. It is one of the most ancient cultivated grains and represents strength, power, and victory in battle. Pagans ask the Barley Moon to bring vigor, prosperity, and health to their communities. This is the time to harvest and dry medicinal and aromatic herbs for the rest of the year. To ensure prosperity for one's house for the entire year, custom dictates that you make a bouquet of seven ears of wheat harvested on the seventh day of the seventh month at the seventh hour.

This Moon's energies are dynamic and her intense spiritual flow is a reference to storms and lightning. These natural elements are present in many mythologies (Greek, Scandinavian, Native American, Siberian, Viking) and represent the power of the Sky. The Thunder Moon reconnects you to your childhood fears and sends light down violently into the darkness of night. She reveals your buried fears while giving you the opportunity to take control of them. This is a Moon who brings you revelations about yourself. In the heart of summer, nature has unfurled its beauty and gives answers to those who know how to listen to them.

As storms descend to your depths beneath the rays of this Moon, allow the thunder to resonate in your chest and make your soul vibrate. Let the flash of lightning bring your darkest parts into the light. Where have you hidden your fears? Where have your terrors shut themselves away? Do you really want to be rid of them? What can you put in place to allow this transformation to take place?

JULY ○ PLANT SPIRIT
YARROW

NAMES: Yarrow (*Achillea millefolium*) is also known as nosebleed plant, soldier's woundwort, milfoil, and thousand-leaf. It is a member of the St. John's group of healing herbs.

IT GROWS throughout Europe and Asia on trails and hills and in pastures, prairies, and sunny areas. It blooms from June until the end of autumn. Its flowered tops are harvested in summer from July to September.

PROPERTIES: Yarrow is a hemostatic plant *par excellence* and has been part of the pharmacopoeia since Antiquity. It also regulates digestion, promotes venous circulation, and has a positive impact on the liver. Known for soothing cramps, it is an effective antispasmodic during menstruation and Hildegarde de Bingen described it as a helpful treatment for menstrual problems and excessive bleeding. It should not be consumed by children or women who are pregnant or breastfeeding because of its abortive properties. Yarrow is a pillar of Celtic herbalism and Chinese medicine. It is often given to people struggling with depression because it has an effect on persistent sadness and dark thoughts, in part thanks to its ability to reconnect to inner courage.

SYMBOLISM Yarrow's name comes from Achilles, the Greek hero who learned about this plant's benefits from Chiron the centaur, who had used yarrow's hemostatic powers to care for wounded warriors during the Trojan War. Yarrow is considered a witch's herb and is used in magical rituals and to purify divination tools. Its ability to keep sinister spirits at bay is widely recognized and it is one of the plants kept on hand during exorcisms. As tombs dating from 200,000 years ago have revealed, yarrow was also used as an offering. More importantly, it is a plant oracle that develops intuition and can be used for divination. In the I Ching, or ancient Chinese divination text, yarrow stalks are used as prophecy sticks. Women who asked it questions under the light of the Full Moon were said to have access to knowledge of their romantic future. Yarrow corresponds with the Water and Air elements and the number seven, which is sacred in many traditions.

JULY ○ FEMININE ARCHETYPE

MAWU

THE ENLIGHTENED AND SERENE WOMAN

This goddess myth comes from African cosmogonies. Her cult took root in West Africa and spread all the way to Brazil. She is depicted either as the feminine ideal, in the company of her twin brother Lisa, or as a double androgynous goddess named Mawu-Lisa who is both man and woman. She embodies the Moon and her brother the Sun.

Together they form the creator couple, two sides of the same coin. She conveys all of the feminine elements found in the yin of Eastern philosophy: gentleness, cold, rest, night, earth, and obscurity. Myths describe her carrying the cosmic egg that created Earth and being helped by a serpent who ensures the security of the heavenly world. As a mother goddess she carries creation and reigns over the vault of the heavens and the land of humanity by carefully guiding the human soul. She represents wisdom and knowledge.

THE GODDESS OF WISDOM

Work with Mawu and explore your body as a space: a creative, receptive, and emotive space. Vibrate to the influences of this stimulating month. When these energies pass through your body, Mawu brings you knowledge of yourself. Allow your body to relax, unfold, and open like the rest of nature during summer. Welcome your vigor with gentleness and giving yourself the possibility to concretize your desires to do and be different things. Mawu brings you the wisdom to care for your inner ecology. This is the time to let yourself be carried by the fire of summer and the sweet coolness of the Moon. Radiate in abundance and take your rightful place in this world.

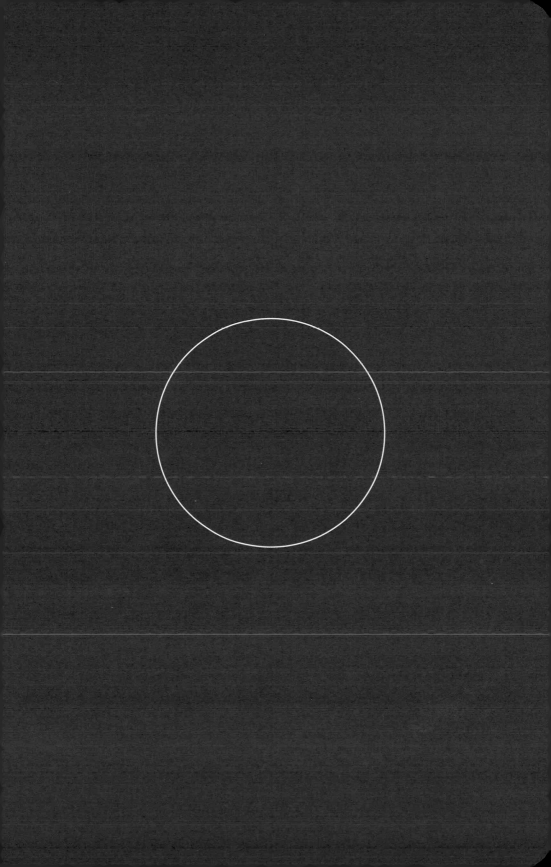

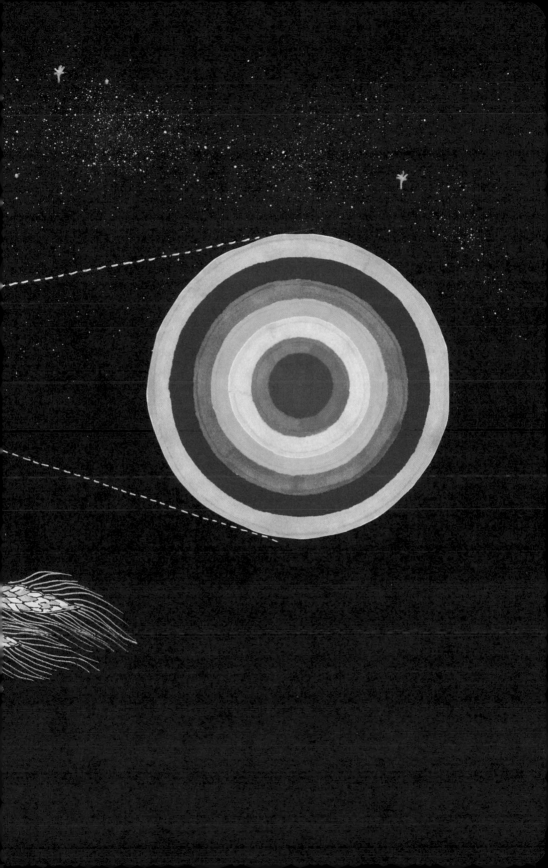

AUGUST
CELEBRATING PROSPERITY

AUGUST ○ FULL MOON
ABUNDANCE

Under this Full Moon, we honor our Earth. The natural world around us is at its most generous. Accept this richness and enjoy this time of pleasure and gratitude. Exercise your ability to live in the present moment and reconnect yourself to the world with your five senses. Be attentive to the sensations, odors, fragrances, and sounds around you. Celebrate abundance by mindfully tasting nature's gifts. To take full advantage of this time you must know how to slow down. The Fire element is dominant during this period; be careful to avoid excess. Adjust your concept of time and listen to your body because it knows what rhythm you should take. Play with your senses and learn to look with your hands by touching soil, grass, bark, and skin. Savor the night and look up at the heavens. The Moon invites you to enter into conversation with the Earth. She brings you a kind of healing by reweaving the bond with your inner temple and this restoration will keep you going for the next six months. This is also a time to look ahead. Be who you want to be and assume your truest nature. You have been in a phase of apprenticeship up until now but with the August Full Moon you begin a phase of going deeper into what you have learned.

Like July, August is often a time of solar or lunar eclipses. The powerful energies of these eclipses work deep within you to heighten your sensations and reveal what is buried inside. While the idea of the solar eclipse is to allow things you have consciously pushed away to surface, during a lunar eclipse the aim is to reveal what your subconscious has repressed. Using this symbolism, you can clean out your past, bad habits, toxic bonds, and harmful schemas.

SVADHISTHANA CHAKRA is a sacral chakra situated a few inches below the navel in the zone just above the genital organs. Meditate with the mantra of the August Full Moon while concentrating on the second chakra. Feel its orange light grow brighter and spread throughout this area of your body.

MANTRA: "I give thanks for life in all its forms."
INTENTIONS: I give thanks to the Full Moon. May she continue to make my harvests fruitful and may she open my heart to gratitude.

ABUNDANCE RITUAL FOR HONORING THE EARTH AND MOON

Harvest or purchase a piece of fresh fruit and a few fresh or dried vervain leaves to bless the Earth.
Perform this ritual outdoors in nature. It will be more powerful.
Open the circle.
Look at the Full Moon, take the fruit in your hands and bring it up the heart chakra. It represents your offering and unifies the Earth and Sky.
Thank the Moon for her gifts. Set your intentions of abundance for the coming season.
Eat half of the fruit and bury the rest in the ground. If the fruit has a pit, place it in the ground. Finish by covering with the vervain leaves.
Close the circle.

AUGUST ● NEW MOON
RADIANCE

Energies are active during this period because the days are longer, but it is still a time for contemplation. Know how to slow down, redefine your rhythm, and feel free from any hindrance. Let your energy radiate, reinforce your confidence, and let your feminine power glow. By opening yourself to internal clarity you will acquire greater personal strength and determination. The New Moon pushes you to gently assert yourself without judgement, without guilt, and rejoicing in your creative abilities. She offers you the chance to become your own light source and propels you toward independence.

With the radiance centered in your chest at the heart chakra, you will reassess your professional, familial, and personal relationships with others. This reevaluation of your human ties will open you to profound modifications and making new choices. With the August New Moon, you connect directly to your instinct and can let yourself be guided. Listen to the path of your heart.

ANAHATA CHAKRA is the heart chakra located in the center of the chest. Meditate with the mantra of the August New Moon while concentrating on the fourth chakra. Feel its green light grow brighter and spread throughout this area of your body.
MANTRA: "I nourish my inner flame with love."
INTENTIONS: In myself I find the resources I need to create the life I want. I am radiant because I have confidence in myself.

GOLDEN HANDS RITUAL
Open the circle.
Sit down alone and rub your hands together until you start to feel energy circulating.
Clasp your hands together in front of you and then open them to the Sky. Now imagine two round and shining Moons in the centers of your palms and place your hands on your chest at the heart chakra.
Call upon the goddess Ishtar and ask her to radiate within you and allow your feminine power to take its rightful place.
Feel the energy circulating. Set your intentions.
Place your open hands in front of you once more and observe that energy is now diffusing around you.
Close the circle.

AUGUST ○ WITCH'S MOON
HARVEST
THE TIME OF BENEDICTIONS

The August moon gets its Harvest Moon name from the golden color of wheat. She is linked to fertility and has a vast field of activity because she brings both material abundance through the harvest and spiritual abundance through self-fulfillment. She invites you to enjoy this, be thankful for it, revitalize, and grow in strength, creativity, and motivation.

She is connected to the Earth and indicates a time to take stock of what you have learned, think about how to develop it further, and prepare new harvests. In a more tangible sense, this is the moment to harvest and dry herbs that will remind you of these hot days bursting with energy for the second half of the year. Under this lunar influence you will follow the path to your origin and the heart of your innermost self.

Enjoy the fruits of what you prepared in March during the Crow Moon, when you brought out the seeds you kept safe during the fall and winter. The wheel of seasons has turned and here you are under this Moon, about to harvest what you will dry and protect for the next six months. This sense that a cycle is ending is especially strong during the last days of August and this gives you a chance to make a new start even though energies are beginning to decrease. This Moon connects you to the past and future, so make sure you are anchored in the present. Look at the six months that have gone by to find the lessons your journey has taught you. Learn to find abundance in everything so that even difficult things can be seen as important experiences. The idea of a cycle, of both death and resurrection, is at the core of the Harvest Moon.

Beneath the powerful energies of the Harvest Moon, take a step back and pause to think. Examine your personal harvests. What you have dedicated yourself to for the past several months is now up for review. What will your first harvest be? In the same way you give thanks to nature, honor your own efforts and potential and be aware of how far you have already come.

AUGUST ○ PAGAN FESTIVAL
LUGHNASADH
JULY 31–AUGUST 1

This major Sabbat is often called "Lammas" and is present in Celtic, Anglo-Saxon, and Native American cultures, to mention only a few.

For the Hopi tribe, August is the month of the snake dance, a ritual of death and rebirth: the men dance with live snakes in their mouths to ask the gods to bring fertility to the community. It is a time when humanity chooses to celebrate nature and its abundance with joy and sharing, often around a meal. Lughnasadh is the first of three harvest festivals and is followed by Mabon, a celebration of the mid-harvest (autumn equinox), and Samhain, the last harvest of the year (October 31st). It pays homage to Mother Earth's generosity and the festival energies that are at their peak. This is a season of profound gratitude when you can understand your bond to the Earth in a tangible way and admire—with hope—the harvests that communities will depend on for survival in the months to come.

This festival is the climax of the season between the summer solstice and the autumn equinox and is a transition between the ascending and burning energies of summer and the descending and prescient energies of autumn. This is a time of transformation, a portal between ending and beginning during which you observe the changes taking place in nature as well as those taking place in your life.

To celebrate your union with the Earth and your reconnection to yourself, use your hands and their creative power. Knead bread that will become round and golden like the Sun to honor its light. Roman priestesses practiced this ritual by baking moon bread as an offering to Diana. The host in the Catholic religion is a continuation of this motif. Meditate with your hands clasped together, dance hand in hand with others, and give free rein to natural creations like flower garlands or rock mandalas. Collect natural objects that will enrich your altar after being charged in the solar energies of the season: driftwood, meditation sticks, stones, shells, dried flowers, feathers, leaves, etc.

ANCESTRAL BREAD RITUAL
You will need ⅔ cup (140 g) organic wheat flour, ¾ cup (150 g) organic corn flour, 2¼ teaspoons (7 g) instant yeast, 1 teaspoon salt, 2 teaspoons sugar, 2 eggs, ½ cup (100 g) melted butter, and 8½ fluid ounces (250 ml) milk. You will use an oven preheated to 350°F (180°C), a round dish, and incense. Your round loaf made from corn flour is a symbol of the Sun, the Wheel of the Year, and the chakras.
Open the circle and, if you wish, burn the incense to incarnate the Sun. Its energetic properties are calming and harmonizing.

Mix together the flours and yeast.

In another bowl, beat the eggs while adding the sugar, salt, melted butter, and milk. Combine with the dry ingredients.

Pour the mixture into a mold and bake for 45 minutes.

Finish by giving thanks to nature and close the circle.

Serve the bread warm during a shared meal. Set aside a piece to give back to the Earth as an offering.

AUGUST ○ PLANT SPIRIT
VERVAIN

NAMES: Vervain (*Verbena officinalis*) is also known as the holy herb, simpler's joy, and herb of the cross.

IT GROWS primarily in Europe, North Africa, and Asia and can reach up to thirty inches in height. Its pink or blue flowers grow in spikes. It is often found along trails, outside forests, and in hilly areas. Vervain is filled with high energies and is ready to harvest when it blooms under a summer New Moon and when Sirius—a mythical star important in Greek and Egyptian cultures—is rising.

PROPERTIES: Along with mistletoe, selago, and samolus, vervain is one of four foundational medicinal plants that have been used since Antiquity. The druids used to add it to their lustral water. Vervain is a panacea known for its digestive benefits and is effective for calming anxiety and promoting relaxation. It can also be administered during a fever. Pregnant women are advised against using it.

SYMBOLISM: Romans associated this plant with Venus, goddess of love. It became an ingredient in love potions, and anyone who drank or ate its leaves risked being bewitched. By extension, vervain was believed to protect the home and bring good luck. It was used to bless festival sites as well as marriage banquets, and leaves were often slipped into children's pockets or shoes to ensure their good fortune and health.

Its evocative names in French (sorcerer's herb, enchantment herb) are evidence of its connection to magical practices. Vervain facilitates divination and prophecy and stimulates creativity. It has also been used to purify altars.

AUGUST ○ FEMININE ARCHETYPE

ISHTAR

THE FIERCE WOMAN

Also called Inanna, this Mesopotamian deity was one of Antiquity's most important goddesses. She was revered by the Babylonians and Assyrians as an astral deity and was symbolized by a star with eight branches as early as 3,000 BC. She was the daughter of Sin, the moon god, but she gradually took his place as the primary lunar deity. Her cult spread to several different regions and she has various names in each place. She also shares characteristics later seen in Venus, Aphrodite, and Demeter.

Ishtar is incredibly radiant because she personifies the woman in every stage of her expansion: seduction, joy, and fertility. She is a free woman, a lioness, and a "virgin" goddess in the original sense of the word: sexually experienced and independent from all male domination. She represents feminine desire, and votive objects like gold and silver yonis were often dedicated to her. In the patriarchal universe of the time, she broke with convention and stood before men without apologizing for her contradictions: she embodies love but also enjoys war and confrontation. The yin-yang polarities are quite pronounced in Ishtar and she was often referred to as both male and female. She does not have a divine masculine equivalent, but her very positive image of flourishing and fertility at times grows dark, embodying the sacred prostitute or witch. Her myth is part of this duality: as a moon goddess she is capable of giving life and taking it away. It is said that Ishtar descended into the underworld to overthrow her sister, the evil Ereshkigal, goddess of the underworld.

During her descent into hell she passed through seven doors corresponding to the seven days of the waning Moon. At each door she was stripped of something she was wearing until she was naked, like the Black Moon. These doors represent profound transformation and the layers you leave behind. In hell she became a prisoner, and her absence on Earth brought about desolation. The world was sinking into an abyss and demanded that Ishtar be freed. She was not allowed to leave unless someone else was given in exchange. Her lover took her place in hell and was permitted to see her for part of the year in spring and summer.

THE GODDESS OF SACRED SEXUALITY

Ishtar is the star you should follow to find the path of your sexuality and independence. Feel her awaken the fiery energy sleeping in the hollow of your belly. With her help, activate the powerful kundalini, a vital sexual force envisioned as a snake coiled at the base of your spine. Shed yourself of unneeded layers and comments from the outside and dance naked, celebrating the beauty of your body. Through Ishtar, find the wild woman that you are. Listen to your desire. You deserve love.

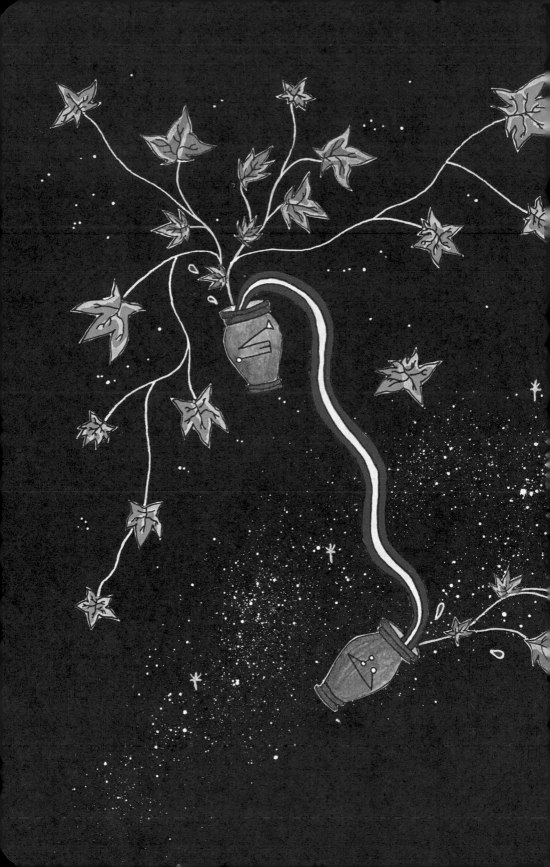

SEPTEMBER

THE BALANCE
OF FORCES

BALANCE

On this September Full Moon, reconnect to all aspects of your life and take stock before the start of a new year. This is a reentry point—albeit a symbolic one—that prompts you to consider your first harvests. Look at what actions you have taken in the last six months and observe the results objectively. This is the time to become more balanced and feel the shadow part and the light part in both your body and spirit. This Moon requires you to work with your yin and yang. Examine what seems to be out of harmony and open your heart to the emotions that come up. This path concerns every aspect of your life, including your sexuality. After a season of opening to your every desire, now make an adjustment to give and receive in equal measure. What are your desires? How do you experience pleasure? This time of deep restructuring is necessary.

You may feel very emotive under this Moon, but let the surge come up. Don't judge yourself too harshly and leave rigidity at the door. Accept your contradictions because they can also be your greatest strength. If you accept that you are vulnerable, you become authentic. Learn to listen to your body because it knows how to talk to you. In September your attention should be focused on the throat—the door to the lungs and the organ of autumn in Chinese medicine—and the thymus. Together they reinforce your ability to resist external aggressions. This Moon liberates your words while teaching you how to converse in an authentic and balanced way. Every word contains a vibration that you must harmonize with in order to fully live your truth.

VISHUDDHA CHAKRA is the throat chakra. Meditate with the mantra of the September Full Moon while concentrating on the fifth chakra. Feel its blue light grow brighter and spread throughout this area of your body.
MANTRA: "The medicine of words is acting within me."
INTENTIONS: I am balancing my masculine and feminine parts. I seek harmony and truth.

INSTINCTIVE CHANT RITUAL

Take out your instruments (Tibetan singing bowls, drums, kalimbas, koshi chimes) or make your own with what you have on hand (bells, a rain stick, etc.).

Open the circle.

Under the Full Moon, reconnect to the goddess Isis and ask her to bring you balance, something she embodies more than anyone else because she knows the paths of death and life.

Pick up an instrument that speaks to you, let your intuition guide you, and play from your heart.

When the moment is right, let sounds, instinctive or sacred chants, mantras, or kotodama phrases emerge from your mouth. Have confidence in your belly. Let your voice rise up to the Moon.

Sing and play as much as you desire. Close the circle.

SEPTEMBER ● NEW MOON
PURIFICATION

We continue our deep cleansing with the energies of the September Full Moon. After the fire of summer, the Water element linked to autumn comes to wet the coals that are still burning from the previous season. Much is asked of you during this time, but go into your body and use the dynamic energies of summer to gradually bring your own energy from the outside to the inside. When the body is in alignment the mind will follow. Offer it the possibility of entering a new dynamic, one that is less intense but more regular and constant. If you don't already practice one, begin an activity that balances the mind and body; this is truly the ideal time to start. To avoid the emotional rollercoasters and immense fatigue caused by the powerful energetic cleansing of this New Moon, take care of yourself and be patient. This is the key to your stability. Reconnect with the earth to strengthen your anchor and relieve yourself of what is no longer beneficial to you in symbolic water. This process takes place in the lower half of the body and the first chakra, your seat of stability. You cannot rise if your roots are not firmly planted. In the same way you do this with your body, it is essential to also purify your home and sacred spaces.

MULADHARA CHAKRA is the root chakra located in the perineal area. Meditate with the mantra of the September New Moon while concentrating on the first chakra. Feel its red light grow brighter and spread throughout this area of your body.
MANTRA: "My roots dive into Mother Earth. Her energy rises up within me and allows me to lighten my load."
INTENTIONS: This new cycle is an invitation to purify my body, mind, and home. I direct my thoughts toward my sacred temple. I make time for myself.

ERASING RITUAL

You will need a bowl, some water, a sheet of paper, and a fountain pen.
Open the circle.
After using one of your purifiers (burning herbs or palo santo) to cleanse the space, wave some of the smoke around you.
Concentrate on writing down what you would like to be rid of, starting your sentences with, "I liberate myself from . . ."
When you have completed the list of things you want to banish from your life, plunge the paper into the water until the sentences blur. This may take several hours, so close the circle and let the words slowly disappear.
Give the water back to the Earth when you think the work of erasure has ended.

SEPTEMBER ○ WITCH'S MOON
HORNED ☆ HUNTER
THE DOOR TO THE DARK SEASON

This Moon is called the Hunter's Moon or Horned Moon and for pagans she represents the entrance to winter and a time when daily life is spent preparing to welcome the cold and enjoying a certain nostalgia.

Associated with abundance, this Moon tells us it is time to bring in the firewood and the harvest, jar our produce, and dry out the last herbs.

She shines between two movements, one turned toward summer, the other toward winter. She invites you to take part in a major cleansing of your living spaces—sorting, putting away, purifying—to make room for an exploration of your inner world.

Native Americans associate this Moon with hunting because her appearance meant it was time to prepare winter stores. She also bears the name the Horned Moon as a reference to the buck deer, god of the forest and a soul guide. This animal represents an ancient protective deity. As a psychopomp it guides the dead, and its antlers symbolize the cycle of life.

By the light of this Hunter's Moon you often find yourself overcome by a sometimes inexplicable sadness and nostalgia. Welcome these emotions with kindness as they color your daily life. What are they trying to reveal? This Moon teaches us that sometimes sadness is a season, that energies touch us in order to heal us. What wound do you need to tend to? Give thanks to the timeless wisdom of the Moon and the way she leads you to examine yourself so you can enter the dark season in peace.

SEPTEMBER ○ PAGAN FESTIVAL
MABON
SEPTEMBER 21–22

This is the second of the three harvest festivals and takes place between Lughnasadh and Samhain. It represents the sacred time of harvest as well as equilibrium in nature and is celebrated during the autumn equinox, when day and night are of equal length. The next day you enter a period of darkness but also one of softness and detachment. For the community, this festival was a transitional time to appraise the harvest that would get them through the winter. Symbolically, it is a time to enjoy the fruits of your labor, to honor your "sacrifices," and gather together at events that bring you closer to your community. You are no longer in a period of openness to new things, but instead one of consolidation of what we have gained and reinforcement of ties to other people. This celebration honors your harvests and invites you to close chapters in your life. Make concrete decisions, put an end to a relationship, or free yourself from a life schema you no longer want. Balance will come spontaneously, between harvest and abandoning.

This is also the time to prepare for the coming season by jarring fruits and vegetables or making jams and jellies. These preparations are a counterbalance to the longer nights, the beginning of the darkest time of year, and the calming of high energies linked to the fires of summer. The equinox is a portal that invites you to examine your life and reestablish balance in every area. In the same way that nature is starting to slow down, so are you.

CROWN RITUAL

You will need a few branches of ivy, wire, and string made from natural fibers.

You can perform this ritual in groups to celebrate Mabon.

Open the circle.

Make crowns representing the sacred circle of seasons. Ivy symbolizes equilibrium, stability, and the deepening of bonds.

Wind the ivy branches around a circle of wire and secure them with the string.

Give thanks to nature and the spirit of the ivy. Close the circle.

These crowns can be worn or used to decorate your altar.

SEPTEMBER ○ PLANT SPIRIT
GROUND IVY

NAMES: Ground ivy (*Glechoma hederacea*) is also known as gill-over-the-ground, creeping charlie, alehoof, and field balm. It is part of the St. John's group of healing herbs.

IT FLOWERS between March and October. This creeping and persistent plant is widespread in temperate zones of Europe, North America, and Asia, where it grows on tree trunks and rocks.

PROPERTIES: Ground ivy is an excellent tonic and has antiscorbutic and vulnerary properties. Every part of this little ivy plant is good, earning it the name "master of all" in French. The long branches can be used for crowns.

SYMBOLISM: Ground ivy is always green and represents rebirth, the link between life and death, and eternal life. For this reason, it was often associated with the immortal Osiris. It is found in many cultures as a good luck charm. Because it evokes perseverance and stability it is a perfect symbol for long-lasting emotional bonds: young people look-ing for love used to slip a leaf under their pillow and newlyweds were crowned with braided ivy. Crowns are also found in druidic ceremonies in which ivy is featured as a duplicitous goddess who gives gifts and takes them away as part of the cycle of life. Its leaves are sacred and linked to the moon goddess because they promote prophecy and the search for self. Ground ivy's strong connection to the Earth and stones make it a symbol of putting down roots and deepening emotional connections, as well as sometimes suffocation.

SEPTEMBER ○ FEMININE ARCHETYPE
ISIS
THE MAGICIAN

Isis is a primordial goddess, the mother of gods, and a protector of nature and life. Within her she carries an incomparable power that resonates with other times of the year (June, because she is connected to the sign of Cancer, and August when the Leo portal opens and her star, Sirius, aligns with the Earth and Sun to create powerful energies mirroring your life path). In September she is usually associated with the balance she embodies as a double deity, both nurturing and destructive, on the fence between death—a force she rubs shoulders with and defies—and life, which she symbolizes as a mother goddess. She is a representation of profound femininity and a protector of childbirth. One of the sacred Egyptian symbols associated with her is the Isaic knot. Also called the "blood of Isis" or "tyet," this is a very powerful magical protection sign that women in labor wore to help births go smoothly. Born after three brothers on the fourth day of Creation, Isis is closely linked to the four lunar phases and the four seasons.

She is also attached to the Water element and the Nile River and so was logically associated with the sea and the flow of emotions. Isis was worshipped by one of the largest esoteric cults in history that spread beyond the borders of Egypt and extended to Greece and the Roman Empire. In these places she represented wisdom, Earth, and the Moon. Statues depicting her as a black goddess were portrayals of lunar eclipses. In Greece she completely supplanted the moon god and was connected to secret initiation practices. These ceremonies were called "mysteries of Isis." Isis has carried this occult dimension ever since the beginnings of her myth as a "great magician" when she managed to put the pieces of her husband Osiris's body back together to bring him back to life. A "rememberment," which is not so far from the word "remember." With her help, the past can help you reconstruct the future and memory is a cement you can use to find and reassemble yourself.

THE GODDESS OF CREATIVE POWER

Let yourself be penetrated by the mystery of the phrase engraved on a stone beneath a portrait of Isis: "I am all that hath been, and is, and shall be; and my veil no mortal has hitherto raised." This guardian of deep femininity invites you to let a secret dimension enter your life. Accept the mystery that is hidden in all things. Cultivate your mystery and glorify the powerfully creative woman magician that you are. Fertilize your secret garden and nourish it with your past experiences, welcoming the infinite possibilities to come. Watch this garden flourish in the silence of your inner temple. Discover the importance of ritual. Isis unites you with your spiritual dimension; open your soul to the invisible world.

OCTOBER

THE SOURCE OF INTERIORITY

The first frosts drive us to walk in the direction of our internal lands and this Moon asks you to examine the link between life and death. She reveals the mysteries of cycles by offering you the chance to reconnect to your essence. Reconnect your body and soul at every level by diving into the deepest part of yourself. Continue the cleansing that began with the September Full Moon and let die whatever needs to leave to start the process of rebirth. This Moon symbolizes passing and invites you to make changes connected to your deepest and innermost desires. Reconnect to your internal compass and your instinct. It will help you heal whatever is preventing you from being wholly yourself, so give yourself permission to grieve in a healthy way. During the previous Moons you have concentrated your energies toward the Earth, and now that you are firmly anchored, lift your energies and give yourself completely to this magnificent spiritual voyage of intuitive discovery. Focus your meditation practice on the third eye because it is the door to inner communication.

AJNA CHAKRA, the third eye and intuition center, is located in the middle of the forehead between the eyebrows. Meditate with the mantra of the October Full Moon while concentrating on the sixth chakra. Feel its indigo light grow brighter and spread throughout this area of your body.

MANTRA: "I am connected to my source and have confidence in my intuition."

INTENTIONS: I experience this Moon as a rite of passage, leaving behind what must die so I can be reborn.

INTERNAL RIVER RITUAL

You will need a few anchoring stones like granite and protective stones like tiger's eye or obsidian.

Open the circle.

Sit down and take the stones in your hands.

After a few breaths, concentrate on the point in the center of your forehead between your eyebrows.

Imagine there is a door in this spot: open it and go down a flight of stairs. At the bottom is a river that has to be crossed, and to do this you must leave behind what you do not need and what cannot pass over to the other side of the river. Depending on the person, these might be things like clothing, a bag, a lock of hair, a bone, a pebble, an emotion, a sadness, another person, etc.

When you are ready, slip into the current. Cross the river and once you are on the other side give thanks to the water medicine for this rebirth.

Close the circle.

OCTOBER ● NEW MOON
EVOLUTION

The New Moon this month works to balance your relationships. With one hand you tighten the deep bonds you have with your "clan," and with the other you cut ties and take distance. Driven by your quest for truth and harmony, purge your life of any relationship you feel is suffocating you. The separation may be difficult, but this is the path of the liberated woman. Sometimes you must leave something in order to grow. It is by courageously taking this step that you will reach a new stage in your personal and spiritual journey, elevating yourself and growing in wisdom. This Moon of evolution helps you break down the barriers that hold you back and you can rely on the solar plexus chakra for vital energy that will bring you willpower, mastery, and assurance.

MANIPURA CHAKRA is the center of the solar plexus. Meditate with the mantra of the October New Moon while concentrating on the third chakra. Feel its golden yellow light grow brighter and spread throughout this area of your body.

MANTRA: "I make choices that are not guided by fear."

INTENTIONS: I am consciously taking the path of my own existence in hand; I am joining my clan.

SHAMANIC PLANTS RITUAL

To perform this cleansing rite, use either a mixture of dried sacred plants containing sage and a small charcoal burner or a smudge stick and an abalone shell. You will need a feather, too.

Open the circle.

Set an intention to purify your body, living space, crystals, and spiritual objects.

Begin by burning the plants. When they start to give off a lot of smoke, use the feather to waft it toward you to cleanse your body.

Open a window and pass through each room with the plants. Turn counter-clockwise because lunar direction chases away negativity. End at the entrance to your home. If there are multiple floors, begin in the room at the highest elevation. Return to your altar and pass your stones and objects through the smoke.

When the purification is finished, close the circle.

OCTOBER ○ WITCH'S MOON

BLOOD ☆ LEAF

CELEBRATING THE HOME

In witchcraft tradition this Moon is connected to blood: the blood of animals slaughtered for curing before winter and that of your bloodline. You are entering a period of preparation. The cold season and dark nights are coming and now is the time to turn inward to your own inner living space. Prepare a cocoon to welcome in your own presence during these months, decorate your altar with natural elements that are still present, and dry the last herbs. This Leaf Moon marks the final harvest and announces a moment of spiritual growth. She symbolizes the home and family and turns us definitively in the direction of our interior and our interiority.

Under the auspices of the Blood Moon, close your eyes and travel inside yourself, seeking harmony. Listen to the beating of your heart and know that the blood pumping in your body is life. It holds the history of your lineage and the memories of your matrilineal line. Receive this legacy like a treasure. Use this force to construct your cocoon, consolidate your interior ecology, and feel like one woman among many. What can you honor in this bond to your ancestors? How can you connect spiritually to all of the women from the dawn of time?

SAMHAIN

OCTOBER 31–NOVEMBER 1

This festival falls between the spring equinox and the winter solstice and is the last of the harvest festivals. It serves as a prelude to winter while the Earth prepares to confront the cold and marks the end and the beginning of the Celtic year. It is a stage of deep connection to the mystical world. With the lengthening of the previous months, Samhain allows you to meditate on the year that has passed and consider what was beneficial and what was not; this is the final assessment of your harvests. Even though Samhain was rebaptized as "All Saints' Day" in the ninth century, this festival still possesses its spiritual aura as a portal between the immaterial and physical worlds.

This night is the sacred passage of shadow and silence, death and rebirth. Vibrational energies are very high. It is a night associated with Crone, the old woman triple moon goddess, who in the pagan tradition opens us to divination and wisdom. We see beyond the worlds and connect to the totality of the cycle of life, destruction and rebirth. Symbolically the Goddess is returning to Mother Earth's belly to die before regerminating. This night is a time to honor your ancestors and your lineage by lighting candles to guide their souls and making offerings to the Earth. In the silence and connections of the invisible world, you are passing through the veil of what is inexpressible.

ANCESTOR RITUAL

You will need a few candles, a spool of white thread, and a pair of scissors.

Honor your ancestors. This ritual can be performed in a group or with family members.

Open the circle.

Light the candles. Call upon Ix Chel, goddess of weaving and life cycles, and ask her to help connect you to your ancestors.

Take the spool of white thread and unwind it as you speak the first names of the people in your matriarchal and patriarchal line: "I am . . . mother of . . . daughter of . . . granddaughter of . . . great-granddaughter of . . . great-great-granddaughter of . . ."

Go as far back as your memory allows.

When you have finished, cut the thread. Tie the two ends in a knot and seal it with wax from the candle.

Feel that you are part of this circle. Take the time to embrace your emotions.

Bury or burn the thread.

Close the circle.

OCTOBER ○ PLANT SPIRIT
SAGE

NAMES: Common sage (*Salvia officinalis*) is also known as golden sage, holy herb, Dalmatian sage, or kitchen sage. It is part of the St. John's group of healing herbs.

IT GROWS in Mediterranean regions today but is originally from Central Asia. It is found near ruins and in old stone walls and is cultivated in Europe and North America. It blooms from May to July and the best time to harvest it is just before the summer solstice when it is fully charged with energy.

PROPERTIES: Sage is often recommended for digestive and menstrual issues and calms the nervous system while also acting as a tonic and antispasmodic. Women who are pregnant or breastfeeding are discouraged from using it and those with hormone-dependent cancers or epilepsy should also avoid it. It is not called the queen of aromatic plants for nothing: its powerful virtues have been widely recognized since Antiquity and its Latin name *Salvia* comes from the word *salvare*, which means "to save" or "to care for." It is credited with many things including guaranteeing good health, though only when consumed occasionally and not on a regular basis. Sage plays a role in balancing female hormones and was used by the Romans to promote fertility and conception.

SYMBOLISM: Sage is an ingredient in numerous magical preparations. As a symbol of wisdom and healing it was gathered by priests in Ancient Rome and druids used a golden sickle to harvest it. Shamans use it because it amplifies one's ability to travel in other planes. Its greatest virtue is purification and it balances energies while chasing away negativity. Its smoke is used to cleanse living spaces, altars, physical and immaterial bodies, stones, and divination objects. It is also an important part of many Native American rituals.

OCTOBER ○ FEMININE ARCHETYPE
IX CHEL
THE DUAL AND CYCLICAL WOMAN

This Mayan moon goddess, like many other moon goddesses, is depicted with features of women of two different ages. Some suggest that she is a combination of two primordial goddesses, but whether or not that is the case she is still, without a doubt, one of the most important goddesses in the Mayan world. She is portrayed as an old woman wearing a snake on her head, animal bones on her body, and sometimes jaguar claws on the tips of her fingers. In this form she embodies the darker side of the Moon, the waning Moon, and the Black Moon. She is fearsome because she brings death and destruction with her. As a water goddess she is the cause of catastrophe and can send down storms, rain, and floods upon the Earth at any moment. This duality is common among moon goddesses whose powers are in opposition and embody both life and death.

In contrast, the depiction of the young goddess Ix Chel is a Full Moon bathing the world in her majestic light. She does, however, preserve many of the old woman's traits, in particular the connection to water, which she pours out of a jar symbolizing her uterus and a source of fertility. She is the guardian of women's sacred temple, their yoni—the vagina and uterus—and she protects women during pregnancy and birth.

She is the goddess of life cycles, and after giving humanity the art of weaving she also became the goddess of weaving. Her double nature allows her to be at once dark and light. She blesses and heals with her waters and women turn to her to enjoy the benefits of ritual purifying baths, especially after giving birth. It is also through water that she reads into souls and becomes an oracle. In doing so she embodies divination.

THE GODDESS OF SISTERHOOD

Align yourself with the powerful Ix Chel who brings healing, clairvoyance, and protection. Just like her, become a weaver and create bonds between yourself and the outside world. Learn to look kindly upon other women, lose your habits of judgement, and accept the Other in her entirety and in her foreignness. Be aware that when you reproach another person you are in fact criticizing yourself. Listen to the messages of Ix Chel. They will bring you knowledge of the sacred and the divine art of connecting to the world.

NOVEMBER

THE BEAUTY OF TRANSFORMATION

NOVEMBER ○ FULL MOON
ALCHEMY

This is the Full Moon of transformation and high spirituality. It is the time when the seeds harvested this year must be protected until the season of awakening when spring returns. Prepare for tomorrow while being fully anchored in the present. Watch over your inner fields and treat them with gentleness and warmth because this is the season of your transmutation. This principle of alchemy transforms one element into another to reveal authentic creative power. For those who practice it, it is a way of evolving toward complete self-actualization. Alchemy echoes the metamorphoses of the lunar cycle—birth, initiatory death, and rebirth—that require us to slow down and find our roots.

Use this Moon as a time to take care of yourself, matching your tempo to the season's. Live more slowly and take the time you need to assimilate everything that happened during your year, from the challenges you faced to the teachings you received. High lunar vibrations require your energy. To take in these energies, use the strength of your roots. Feel them spreading out from your base and open your first chakra. If you can find a balance between the forces of the Earth and the energies of the heavens, you will be able to develop extrasensory abilities and your dreams will carry powerful messages for tomorrow.

MULADHARA CHAKRA is the root chakra located in the perineum. Meditate with the mantra of the November Full Moon while concentrating on the first chakra. Feel its red light grow brighter and spread throughout this area of your body.

MANTRA: "I connect to Mother Earth, I put my trust in her, and I absorb her rhythm."

INTENTIONS: I am becoming the alchemist of my own existence. I assimilate my experiences in order to transform myself."

SACRED BATH RITUAL

Prepare a ceremonial plant bath. This ancestral practice is deeply connected to vegetal energies and opens a passage to Mother Earth and the plant world. It has the power to reconnect you to your spirituality even though it focuses on the physical body.

Select your plants. Heather, the plant of this month, can be chosen for protection. Add apple for wisdom and connection to the world below, lavender for inner peace and relaxation, and thyme for anchoring to the Earth and inner truth.

Open the sacred space.

After infusing your plants in boiling water, pour the tea into the bathwater or use it to rinse yourself at the end of your shower.

Before getting into the bath, cleanse the room with a purifier (burning herbs or palo santo). Then, set your intentions.

Take your bath in mindfulness and give thanks to the plant medicine before getting out of the water.

Close the circle.

NOVEMBER ● NEW MOON
INTROSPECTION

You are standing before an energetic and symbolic portal. This New Moon invites you to look into yourself and become aware of your potential so you can activate your creativity. It reveals your yin, and you need to know how to embrace it. Recharge your soul through introspection, develop your intuition, and follow the path of alignment. This is a season when everything ripens and brings us the seeds of the future. Embrace the dark night in all its depth and confidently let it descend into your center, because this is where you will find the light you need to illuminate your inner temple. Everything is in you; everything always was. Acknowledge the power you have to be your own light in the darkness. Your third eye lights up and its brightness fills you. You are no longer alone: the goddesses, guides, and allies you have worked with for months are still by your side. You now know that strength comes from your belly. You are its guardian. Tonight, pass over to the other side. Open yourself to this symbolic experience of death and travel between the two worlds to allow precious karmic healings to take place. Take ownership of this creative and mystical part of yourself.

AJNA CHAKRA, the third eye and intuition center, is situated in the middle of the forehead between the eyebrows. Meditate with the mantra of the November New Moon while concentrating on the sixth chakra. Feel its indigo light grow brighter and spread throughout this area of your body.

MANTRA: "My creative power is connected to my imagination."

INTENTIONS: I awaken my creator yin while carefully slowing my rhythm.

THIRD EYE DESCENT RITUAL

You will need your moon journal and a pen.

Open the circle.

Sit down in a meditative posture with your eyes closed. Consciously slow down your breathing.

Ask Lilith, the embodiment of creative power and goddess of the underworld, to accompany you on your descent.

Visualize your third eye in the center of your forehead. You may even feel a warm spot.

Place your hands over the third eye.

Slowly use your hands to bring the third eye down to your uterus. Keep your hands on your belly. Wait.

Open yourself to messages, ideas, new projects, and new desires that may arise now or in the days that follow. Write them down.

Give thanks to the Goddess. Close the circle.

BEAVER ☆ FOG

THE REFUGE OF SILENCE

This Witch's Moon coincides with the end of Samhain and opens the cycle of death. It is sometimes called the Fog Moon or Mourning Moon and represents the hostility of the season to come. By entering into meditation and silence, you will experience powerful moments of divination. For Native Americans, this Beaver Moon was the last action Moon of the calendar year. It is time to be finished with projects and relationships that have come to their end. In shamanism the medicine of the beaver connects Water and Earth, elements of autumn and winter, and invites you to rest and enjoy this season of long nights. The beaver is a builder with foresight that knows how to prepare for the cold. This animal teaches you how to organize and empower yourself to symbolically survive the winter. The passage of this Moon encourages you to finish sorting through the things in your home and give to others what you have too much of. Find a place for your divination objects, the herbs you have dried over the last few months, and your candles. In order to be used they must be put aside in their own spot.

Envelop yourself in the fog of this Moon and pass through it in silence. Like the Native Americans, find refuge by entering into *tiyoweh*, that sacred internal space where you go to withdraw from the noise and fury of the world. Here in this private place, at the base of your uterus, create the space that your small inner voice so badly needs. Abandon yourself to this process without fear. Ask yourself honestly about the place you are giving this primal wisdom in your life.

NOVEMBER ○ PLANT SPIRIT

HEATHER

NAMES: Heather (*Calluna vulgaris*) is also known as Scotch heather.

IT GROWS in the limey soils of maritime zones near forests and sandy areas and blooms from July to September. It can be found from the steppes of Siberia to the Scottish Highlands.

PROPERTIES: Heather has long been known to be a urinary tract purifier. It is a plant with detoxifying, diuretic, and anti-inflammatory properties that also soothes joint problems as an antirheumatic.

SYMBOLISM: In French, heather is called the "elf plant" and is said to cover the highlands to ward off spirits and protect humans from the evil eye. The druids appealed to its benefits to solidify the clan and bring happiness to the community. Because of its protective properties and flexibility, it was used to cover huts and barns and was also used in Scotland to make heather ale. This plant is reinvigorating, purifying, and symbolizes the joy of sharing with others. Heather is a witch's plant par excellence because it is used in the making of brooms. The Romany people see it as a symbol of good luck and use it to make amulets.

NOVEMBER ○ FEMININE ARCHETYPE

THE FREE SPIRIT

For us this name evokes much more than a Mesopotamian mother goddess: Lilith is linked to an inflammatory ancestral legend. She is synonymous with the astrological Black Moon and embodies both a fear thousands of years old and visceral fascination. She navigates in the dark skies with subterranean energies reminiscent of the Moon's waning phase. She is associated with the lion, a symbol of power, and with nocturnal birds like the owl, representing wisdom. In Mesopotamian myths, Lilith is depicted as a raging night demon connected to wind and storms. It is said that she uses her fearsome sexual power to seduce both men and women and gives birth to swarms of evil children. Lilith prefigures the myth of the vampire—who comes out at night, enters people's homes to sexually consume them, and leaves behind a trail of death—and is also associated with the legendary succubus demons who appear as women to seduce men and commit evil acts.

Later, in the esoteric Jewish tradition known as Kabbalah, Lilith was said to predate Eve as Adam's first lover. She refused to submit to male domination and embodied the sacred feminine, rebelling in order to preserve her liberty. She was Adam's equal, made from the same clay, and she refused to bend to patriarchal law. She paid the price when God banished her and, depending on the version of the story, either made her sterile or condemned her to give birth to stillborn babies. From then on, she represented danger, absolute evil, and chaos, an image that endured and eventually made her a companion of the devil and, therefore, a witch. After disappearing for a century, she reemerged in the 1970s as a feminist figure, the image of a free and autonomous woman.

THE UNTAMEABLE GODDESS

Call upon Lilith to give you the courage to free yourself. She knows the power of "no" and gives you the chance to say it in your loudest voice. She holds the torch of feminism; feel how her power pushes you to break your yoke and push the limits. She is a symbol of emancipation and creativity without childbirth and evokes internal feminine power and unfettered sexuality. With her by your side, open the circle of wild women.

DECEMBER

SPIRITUAL ELEVATION

HEALING

The December Full Moon is the last of the calendar year and is always a moment of symbolic closure. She lights our heavens throughout the dark nights, and our inner lights should grow brighter to mirror her. This is the time to take care of others and of yourself, to give and receive. This happens through the heart, with love that is dedicated to healing. This Moon encourages you to develop your own medicine and to know and recognize yourself. It is when you lose sight of this inner path and distance yourself from who you really are that the pit within you begins to open. Physical and psychological disease can slip into this space. Listen to your energetic body. You are responsible for your own health, so put into practice what is good and appropriate for you. The path of healing is complicated and requires you to learn to be grateful for what life has given you, even the difficult moments. Your fears, your chains, and your barriers are there to be lifted. They are challenges that allow you to evolve and develop your inner strength.

ANAHATA CHAKRA is the heart chakra located in the center of the chest. Meditate with the mantra of the December Full Moon while concentrating on the fourth chakra. Feel its green light grow brighter and spread throughout this area of your body.
MANTRA: "I open my heart to love and forgiveness. I give and I receive."
INTENTIONS: I am becoming the creator of my own medicine. I walk in the direction of healing and reflect on the teachings of my past experiences.

HEALING RITUAL
Use an elder branch or dried elderflowers for powerful protection against disease and low or negative energies. You will also need a green candle (the color of magic), herbs, the materials to light a fire, a sheet of paper, and a pencil.
Open the circle.
Light the candle or, if possible, light a fire in the chimney.

Using positive affirmations, write down what you are asking to be healed. This may be a physical ailment or a past memory or relationship.
When you have finished, ask the fire medicine to bring you help.
In a small dish or directly in the hearth, burn the paper and the elder branch. Let them be consumed by the flames.
Give thanks to the herb and fire medicines.
Close the circle.

DECEMBER ● NEW MOON
BELIEF

The way you face this final New Moon colors the year that is about to begin. Energies are acting as mirrors: when they are positive, you will enter the year with thoughtfulness; when these energies are blurry or dark, the beginning of the year will be chaotic. Dare to believe and keep your attention respectfully on the path of self-reflection that this lunar connection is offering you. The New Moon asks you to examine your beliefs and wants to know who you are, how you feel about yourself, and the kind of spiritual life you lead. She invites you to build bridges between your innerness and the heavens because everything is linked. If you are cut off from telluric and cosmic energies you will never fulfill your potential, but when you rely on the spiritual worlds you carry within you, you open the path to self-realization. In order to do this, channel the energies passing through your seventh chakra that descend via the pineal gland and flood you with purifying light. Accept this part of the unknown and use it to rid yourself of low vibrations contained in negative emotions like fear and anger. Leave enough space for your desire to hatch. In this way you can transform beliefs into plans, examine the possibilities, and imagine achieving your goals. These intentions will help you manifest your objectives in the months to come.

SAHASRARA CHAKRA is located at the crown of the head. Meditate with the December New Moon mantra while concentrating on the seventh chakra. Feel its purple light grow brighter and spread throughout this area of your body.

MANTRA: "My physical and energetic bodies are in harmony with the vibrations of the Universe."

INTENTIONS: I embody my beliefs and give them the opportunity to find their place in my life.

AMULET RITUAL

To create your amulet for the year to come, you will need objects from nature like pebbles, crystals, wood, feathers, dried plants, flowers, shells, or seeds as well as air-dry clay.

Open the circle.

Meditate and ask Hecate, goddess of the night, to guide you through your creation by connecting you to the spiritual world.

Create your amulet out of clay and the elements you brought. Let yourself be carried by your creative instinct.

Set your intentions as you make the amulet. It will be there to accompany you for the next twelve months.

Close the circle.

Once your amulet is dry, place it on your altar.

DECEMBER ○ WITCH'S MOON
OAK ☆ LONG NIGHT
LUMINOUS DEATH

This Witch's Moon lights up the darkness, bringing light and heat during a dark time. Winter is beginning and the plant and animal world are going into hibernation. Darkness dominates. But this time of death is also one of rejuvenation: the oak tree symbolizes resistance and the courage needed to confront this season. This Moon also embodies strength, healing, and the *axis mundi* that lifts us up and protects us. She anchors us in the midst of the darkest night and allows us to brave the unknown. Put yourself under her protection and healing power. Maintain your human relationships, friendships, and bonds of love, and make your home a place of regeneration during this somber period. Fire is the key element during this lunar month and brings conviviality and hope. This Witch's Moon also invites you to meditate and raise your level of consciousness. The energies that unite will be those that will shape the coming year: healing, sharing, maintaining the fire, support, and contemplation.

Let yourself be guided by the light of the Moon. She lights up the shadows with her silver rays. When you were young you were afraid of this dark void, but now you wear on your forehead the shining lunar crescent that illuminates your nights. Without fear, let your flame burn brightly; it will never be extinguished. With deep breaths, a position that keeps you anchored to the Earth, and your verticality, become this light, this strength, this star in the constellation of wild women.

DECEMBER ○ PAGAN FESTIVAL
YULE
WINTER SOLSTICE: DECEMBER 21

The winter solstice celebrates Yule, the longest night of the year. Darkness has overtaken the light but only for one night; the next day the nights begin to grow shorter. This celebration is connected to two feminine figures: the mother, because in pagan practices this is when the Goddess gives birth to God, who will grow until the summer solstice, and the old woman, who is embodied by Cailleach, the witch of winter. Death is embraced but this festival also celebrates the advent of the Sun in the midst of the shadows.

This door to winter invites you to change your rhythm and slow down. It is a time of introspection, of symbolically returning to the cave to rest your body and spirit. You are invited to enlarge your own light by honoring your sacred space, either by meditating internally or caring for your altar.

Traditionally, after the house has been purified, one burns the Yule log that had been cut from an oak tree and engraved with symbols earlier in the year. Part of it will be kept to light the log next year. Candles burn throughout this night to symbolize the desire to go toward the light.

SOUL CHANTING RITUAL

Set up a few candles. Choose a song or instrument.

This ritual can be performed in a group.

Begin this ritual in a candlelit room. Open the sacred space.

Place candles around the room, one for each person present and each person you want to invite from a distance.

Light the candles from right to left.

Take the time to contemplate each flame, thinking about the person it represents.

Set your intention that light accompany the path of each person.

Sing or play a little to offer your music to the night and guide the souls toward the light. Close the circle.

DECEMBER ○ PLANT SPIRIT
BLACK ELDER

NAMES: Black elder (*Sambucus nigra*) is also known as the Judas tree, boor tree, elkhorn, and the European elder.

IT GROWS along trails and in yards and hedges in Europe, Asia, and North Africa. It blooms in June and July and the berries arrive in early autumn.

PROPERTIES: Black elder is a cure-all that heals a number of ailments in a similar way to the highly beneficial nettle. It is used to fight colds, fever, and coughing, and is also a diuretic promoting drainage and weight loss. It is not recommended for women who are pregnant or breastfeeding.

SYMBOLISM: Black elder is revered in many traditions and is said to harbor the feminine spirit of a nymph or goddess who presides over the cycles of life. This is why if you pick its berries you must not forget to leave her an offering in return. Black elder is present in a number of protection rituals against disease, the evil eye, and negative intentions. Hiking sticks are made from its wood to keep snakes away and walkers sometimes keep a branch on them to bring luck. Cradles were once built out of elder wood to protect young children, and elderberries were thrown at newlyweds for good fortune. Smoke from burning elder wood was used for cleansing and to keep away bad energy. Black elder is also associated with death and is sometimes called the Judas tree because Christ's cross was made from its wood and Judas is said to have hung himself from the branch of an elder tree. To live through the descent into this period of darkness, a black elder branch was burned the night of Yule. In magic it is used to make wands or flutes. When planted near a house it was also supposed to keep witches at bay.

DECEMBER ○ FEMININE ARCHETYPE
HECATE
THE INTUITIVE WITCH

This Greek goddess represents the waning phase of lunar energy. Her alter egos, Artemis (increasing energy) and Selene (maturity) keep her company in the pantheon. The three of them form a life cycle. Hecate is particularly fascinating because she is the bearer of the old woman's wisdom and maturity but still remains intimately connected to changes and periods of transition or passage. Because of the fertility she brings, Hecate was a deity of nature before becoming a dark goddess. In Greece, her power was invoked during rituals when fires were set around the fields. She is depicted with phallic props like torches, serpents, daggers, and keys. Like Isis and her star Sirius, known as "the Big Dog," Hecate is also associated with dogs because they are faithful animals who show us the way in the darkness.

Hecate brings humanity knowledge, understanding, and material wealth, but she is still synonymous with the great witch figure. She became the object of many esoteric cults and embodies the inner voyage and the role of a guide in developing one's intuition and advancing on paths of divination. At one time there was even a divination tool called Hecate's circle that allowed a person to channel messages by turning the wheel. Though she is a dark archetype, this witch has nevertheless always lit the path for men and women. Statues of her were erected at crossroads and intersections because only she possesses the knowledge of three paths: the path of the heavens, the path of Earth, and the path of hell.

THE GODDESS OF INITIATION

During your inner voyage, ask Hecate—guardian of the knowledge of the world of dreams and nightmares—to guide you. As a sorcerer woman, recognize yourself in her and know how to retreat into your protected space to lick your wounds like a she-wolf. Hecate knows the channels that connect the mysterious world to the incarnate world and she will accompany you to the place where you can revitalize yourself. Offer her your gratitude and she will open you to divinatory understanding. Listen to her voice speak to you in the nature around you. Sharpen your animal senses with her help.

JANUARY

EARTH AT REST

INVOCATION

In the depths of winter's cold nights, the January Full Moon shows her pale face to bring you comfort. Hidden away in the inertia of your snowy and frozen inner kingdom, this space-time is a preparation, a moment of indispensable rest. Like the Earth, you are recharging your energies and gaining protection and strength. This intimate relationship with the Earth makes you think about your commitment to her, which is really a reflection of your commitment to yourself. It is good to create a sacred space for the year that is beginning. A place of refuge where your power can find shelter. The season's outward passivity conceals the work being done underground: you are building the foundations for your year that will take root in your earth-belly. Everything happens through your body. Take care of it, nourish it, and teach it patience, perseverance, and resistance. In this time of great invocation, ask your allies, your guides, the Moon, the Earth, and the Universe to show you the way for the next twelve months and reinforce your inner strength.

SAHASRARA CHAKRA is located at the crown of the head. Meditate with the mantra of the January Full Moon while concentrating on the seventh chakra. Feel its violet light grow brighter and spread throughout this area of your body.
MANTRA: "I am one, I am All."
INTENTIONS: I call upon my guides for light so I can cross through the darkness and recharge myself with positive energy.

TWELVE MONTH TAROT SPREAD RITUAL
You will need a tarot deck, your moon journal, and a pen.
This ritual can be performed either during the first twelve days of January, which symbolically contain the totality of the year, or on the night of the Full Moon and the twelve days that follow it.
Open the circle and call upon Selene, the moon mother goddess. Ask her to give you clairvoyance and to accompany you in your search for messages and visions.

After taking the time to anchor and center yourself, draw one card from the deck each day.

Each of these cards will represent a month of the year. The first for January, the second for February, and onward until the twelfth card for December.

Each day before closing the circle, make a note of what card you drew and the information you glean from reading its interpretation. This will help you map out your year's personal energies.

JANUARY ● NEW MOON
INVOLVEMENT

Under this New Moon in the heart of winter, you begin to feel a creative impulse that renews your joy and brings you a certain physical well-being. You feel free from what may have been holding you back the previous year. Tonight, you are on the threshold of the true new year and can embrace it with confidence. Know how to involve yourself in this renewal and engage with your future wholeheartedly, both in terms of choices you have to make and your will to make your dreams a reality. This is the perfect night to ask that the plans forming in your mind—plans that you may not yet be conscious of or those that are still in a very nebulous state—take on a material dimension. Ideas become projections, projections become plans laid out on paper, and these plans become concrete opportunities in the months to come. The desires you identify beneath the moonlight will become your actions in the spring. Your involvement in this planning time is required by the New Moon and will translate into a greater awareness of your own feelings. Open yourself to all dimensions by looking at life in a new way. Be attentive to the signs that are sent to you, particularly those in the world of dreams. They will have an influence on your personal objectives and ambitions. You are better at following your instinct now; know when to rely on it.

SVADHISTHANA CHAKRA is the sacral chakra located a few inches below the navel, in the area just above the genital organs. Meditate with the mantra of the January New Moon while concentrating on the second chakra. Feel its orange light grow brighter and spread throughout this area of your body.

MANTRA: "I connect to my desire and incarnate it."

INTENTIONS: I am involved in my own life. I open my perceptions to internal and external messages.

DREAM PILLOW RITUAL

You will need some dried thyme to strengthen divination and amplify clairvoyance, a small square pocket made of cotton fabric, and sewing materials to close it.

Open the circle.

As you fill the pocket with dried thyme, ask the herb medicine to guide you through your dreams.

Sew the pocket shut and close the circle.

Place the small herb pillow under your pillow all night. The next day, write down the messages you received in your moon journal.

JANUARY ○ WITCH'S MOON
WOLF ☆ SNOW
THE INDEPENDENCE INSTINCT

This Moon evokes powerful symbols and awakens the she-wolf sleeping within you. Also called the Snow Moon or Cold Moon, she resonates with the first calendar month to unveil the coming year's energetic pathway. She arrives close to Epiphany, a Christian celebration marking the arrival of the three wise men, and is celebrated on the twelfth night after December 25th. This is a special night that puts an end to the wintery reign of the Holly King. It is a time of rituals to honor the incarnation of the divine in matter.

Pagans call it the Wolf Moon because in winter this animal does not hibernate and becomes king of the forest, prowling menacingly nearby when food becomes scarce. By honoring this animal, you can protect yourself from danger. This Moon brings strength and inner security by becoming a symbol of protection and light in the heart of darkness. The wolf remains the uncontested master of the night and is protective and loyal. In shamanic culture it symbolizes unity between death and rebirth and also represents independence within the group.

The wolf reveals your wild nature and encourages you to find your life path so you can shine within your clan.

Under the auspices of this January Moon, follow the wolf's tracks, and embody your deepest and truest nature. While the body is resting, the mind is available to open itself to intimate questioning. What do you wish to incarnate in your daily life? What are the values you want to carry? How can you respect your independence?

JANUARY ○ PLANT SPIRIT
THYME

NAMES: Thyme (*Thymus vulgaris*) is also known as common thyme, German thyme, or garden thyme.

IT GROWS in dry soil and finds what it needs where other plants cannot survive. It does well in arid climates but cannot bear the cold. It is found around the Mediterranean basin and in Central Europe, India, and North America. It flowers between April and June and should be harvested in the middle of the season when it is full of active properties. It can be dried because it is typically used medicinally during the cold period of the year.

PROPERTIES: Thyme is perhaps best known as an aromatic plant, but it has many other interesting properties. It acts primarily in the lungs where it protects the bronchi from colds, flu, and chills. It also helps with digestion and supports concentration and relieves fatigue. The active anti-inflammatory and antiseptic substances it contains have been known about since Antiquity. The Greeks and Romans used it to cleanse their homes by burning it, and the Latin word *thymus* comes from the Greek word *thymos*, literally meaning "fumigation herb." Thyme was also considered an offering. In Egypt, *tham* is one of the herbs used in embalming and mummification rituals. By extension, thyme for a long time was used as an antiseptic in hospitals.

SYMBOLISM: Thyme is used to sanctify altars. Thanks to its purifying properties, it repels negative energies. It is associated with both the Water element (like the Moon) and the Air element, accentuates clair-voyance, and reinforces spiritual connection to the invisible world by acting on the third eye, your intuition center. Images of thyme branches were embroidered on clothing because thyme was known for being a plant of courage. It was believed that the strength of its roots gave it the ability to keep the devil at bay.

JANUARY ○ FEMININE ARCHETYPE
SELENE
THE INCARNATION OF PROFOUND FEMININITY

This moon goddess represents the Full Moon phase in the triad with Artemis and Hecate. She is radiant in long white robes with a crescent moon in her hair and glowing milky skin; she is an incarnation of profound beauty and strength. Selene is the archetype of the all-powerful woman: at once the original mother and a voluptuous lover, she symbolizes fertility like all moon goddesses. She is also the goddess most associated with feminine flour-ishing. She transmits an expanding yin energy that pushes women to radi-ate outward. She embodies love, fidelity to others and to one's principles, and stability. She is a goddess of gentleness who breathes confidence into women and their intuition and transmits messages and visions through dreams. She represents perseverance, balance, and protecting the flame of passion, whether it be for another person or for a project.

THE VISIONARY GODDESS
In the circle of wild women, Selene brings us faith in our femininity. She allows you to see further, radiate beyond your body, and know that the woman you are now is capable of showing others the way. Receive the magnificent gift of the sacred feminine, the glorious and peaceful union of your feminine and masculine parts. Share this precious knowledge with your sisters. You can support, awaken, console, and kindly watch over one another.

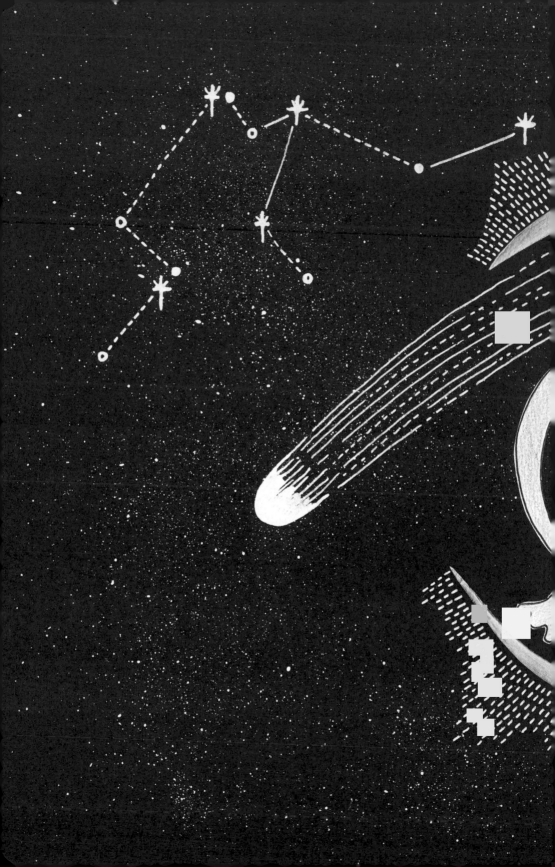

FEBRUARY

A SURGE OF VITALITY

BENEDICTION

We are going to close the energetic year with this very special Full Moon. You have walked the path of twelve Moons and now you have come to receive the February Full Moon's blessing. Beneath her rays, absorb the waves of energy inviting you to unfurl your power. Opening yourself to this magic is a gift. Take care of the light you have brought into yourself. Leave the way open for this light to now spill over into the rest of your life. Anchored in your purified living space and body, make room to welcome this expansion in. Liberate yourself from your fears and reject the resistance that only seeks to interfere with your path. Fear paralyzes the body and mind; let the Moon's energy flow through you to make you more flexible. By filling your third eye chakra with vital energy you will conquer the things standing in your way. Open yourself in joy and gratitude to receive this current of magic abundance. You are now ready to fulfill your potential. Give yourself time to adjust. Offer yourself a period of digestion and recuperation to allow this new intensity to brew in you. Under this Moon you can reclaim your witch's soul, your wild woman body. Make good use of them.

AJNA CHAKRA, the third eye and intuition center, is located in the middle of the forehead between the eyebrows. Meditate with the mantra of the February Full Moon while concentrating on the sixth chakra. Feel its indigo light grow brighter and spread throughout this area of your body.
MANTRA: "I carry the light of life, I am fulfilled."
INTENTIONS: I taste the blessing of this magic Moon to reclaim my personal power.

WITCH'S LADDER RITUAL

You will need three pieces of string, stone pendants, and feathers.
Open the circle. Brigid, the goddess of light, is connected to braiding and will accompany you throughout this ritual.
Center yourself, breathe, and visualize the bond between your third eye and the Moon.

Let the energies descend.

As you welcome lunar benediction, you will begin braiding to create a witch's ladder that will serve as a protective talisman symbolizing the strength of your magic. Braid the three strings together and add the feathers and stone pendants.

Each time you add a stone and knotted feather, tie a knot. At the fourth knot—a number symbolizing the death of self and spiritual rebirth—your ladder will be finished. It will symbolize your power until the next February Full Moon.

Close the circle.

FEBRUARY ● NEW MOON
CLARIFICATION

The New Moon this month offers you greater acuity in your life. As dark as this night may be, it is a blank slate ready to bring you clarity. When you prepare your intentions, try to step outside your mind and simply ask the universe to enlighten you about what is good for you and best for this world. Keep your attention on your crown chakra. Feel the messages being channeled through it. Let your vibration spread freely. Feel free to change your beliefs and align yourself with this New Moon. Be totally present, whatever comes. Avoid mental projections and leave enough space for the true messages of light that will be given to you. Show your gratitude, because giving thanks is the key to opening your soul. Honor everything that has been—the difficult moments and the beautiful times—for the medicine and teaching it brought to your life. Liberate as much inner space as necessary to welcome a renewal.

SAHASRARA CHAKRA is located at the crown of the head. Meditate with the mantra of the February New Moon while concentrating on the seventh chakra. Feel its violet light grow brighter and spread throughout this area of your body.

MANTRA: "I bathe in the pure light of infinity."

INTENTIONS: I open myself to gratitude to offer abundance and clarity in my life.

ROCK SEEING RITUAL

Prepare to receive messages via the intermediary of Mother Earth with this Native American divination ritual.

Find a large irregularly shaped stone and ask its permission before removing it from its natural habitat. Bring along your moon journal.

Open the circle.

Place the stone on the ground in front of you. After meditating, ask it a question. Look at it and concentrate on its surface.

Write down what you see: symbols, letters, silhouettes, animals, plants, faces, geometric shapes, words, etc.

Turn the stone over four times to observe each of its faces and begin the same cycle of observation each time.

At the end, reread what you have written down and establish connections between these things and your original question.

Thank the stone, Mother Earth, and the Moon.

Close the circle. Carefully place the stone back in nature.

FEBRUARY ○ WITCH'S MOON

STORM ☆ DEATH

THE GESTATION PERIOD

This Storm Moon is also called the Death Moon and is above all a time for silence, solitude, and purification. Nature appears to be sleeping and lethargic but is in fact already preparing in its deepest places for rebirth; you are nature's mirror. The storms during this month are spirals of energy you can use to rejuvenate. This is a Moon of internal transformation and requires you to be anchored. It is a time when nature is hostile. Experience the intensity of this external bad weather in your inner place; these forces will feed the warrior woman within you. This is the time to prepare your body to gently leave winter behind and take care of yourself, because this is the only way you will be able to in turn take care of others. You have a duty to respond to your deepest needs so that in the future you can offer the world your generous presence.

Beneath the rays of this Witch's Moon, take a seat and feel nature unveiling its force all around you; the furious wind is demonstrating its power. Calmly take in this energy, for it will nourish your own. You are the only person who can fully support your well-being. Ask yourself how to best care for your internal ecology. Before being reborn on the next Witch's Moon, make sure you have everything you need to begin a new cycle.

FEBRUARY ○ PAGAN FESTIVAL
IMBOLC
FEBRUARY 1 AND 2

Imbolc is a fire festival marking the great return of light. It was originally a Celtic tradition associated with the goddess Brigid, a symbol of fertility whose presence announces the return of the Sun. You are closing the Wheel of the Year and preparing to leave your underground den to return to the bright space. Terrestrial energies are back on track, the first flowers are appearing, and nature is preparing for the sap to rise. Bring out the real and symbolic seeds you have kept all this time during the dark period. This is a time to purify the body and living space.

This ceremony of lights is found in various cultures and time periods. In Ancient Rome, cities were lit with torches for the first week of February. The advent of Christianity erased these pagan rites with Candlemas, a celebration of the Virgin Mary's (or Miriam's) purification forty days after the birth of Christ, but the tradition persisted and even during this Christian celebration people would hold torchlight processions through the streets.

Imbolc was also a time to let out what had been contained all winter during carnivalesque celebrations linked to the Sun. Use this time to cleanse the energy of your house, your altars, and yourself. Place candles in your windows during the two days of the festival.

SMUDGE STICK PURIFICATION RITUAL

You will need rowan wood, a few 6-inch (15 cm) branches of rosemary, lavender, sweetgrass, mugwort, thyme, vervain (plants you are able to harvest near your home and dry), a natural material to tie the plants together, and a pair of scissors.

Prepare to make smudge sticks you will burn to purify your home and yourself. If you have a chimney or stove, burning the rowan wood is a good way to celebrate. It will burn slowly and bring powerful heat while ensuring protection.

Open the circle.

Take the branches and form a bouquet as large as you like, then attach them at the base.

Continue wrapping the string around the smudge stick, squeezing it together as you go. At the top, tie a knot. Use the scissors to cut off any excess string.

Make several smudge sticks for your upcoming rituals. Let them hang to dry then close the circle.

FEBRUARY ○ PLANT SPIRIT
ROWAN

NAMES: The rowan tree (*Sorbus aucuparia*) is also known as the mountain ash, sorb apple, and witch wiggin.

IT GROWS throughout the Indo-European region from Scandinavia to India and the Balkans to Siberia. This tree loves the shade and grows near spruce forests in lower mountain regions. It blooms in May and June and produces fruits in the form of red berries in autumn. It has been used for many years to make a very fine brandy and sour jellies.

PROPERTIES: Rowan relieves problems in the venous system and affects blood circulation. It also has diuretic, antihemorrhagic, and anti-diarrheal properties.

SYMBOLISM: The rowan has a strong connection to superstition and magic. In Celtic culture it is part of the sacred tree calendar and was planted near homes and graves to attract good fortune, repel disease and lightning, and guard the souls of the dead. It was also used to ensure the protection of herds of livestock and animals were often blessed with its branches. Its wood is resistant but easy to carve and was used for sculptures, weaving shuttles, cabinetmaker planes, and bows during the Middle Ages. Rowan wood was often used to make amulets and crosses as well.

In many cultures the rowan is believed to have the same power, life force, and wisdom as the elder tree. Whatever its form—a witch's tree or a walking stick—it gives off the same protective energy and strengthens the divination of whoever uses it in their practices. Rowan sticks, for example, were used to consult oracles.

FEBRUARY ○ FEMININE ARCHETYPE
BRIGID
WOMAN OF FLAMES

Brigid is a Celtic deity whose cult spread throughout Ireland. She was born with a crown of fire, incarnating the flame of life, and is associated with the pagan festival of Imbolc. With the arrival of Christianity, she became Bridget, patron saint of Ireland. As a triple goddess linked to the shamrock, or three-leaf clover, she represents a woman's three ages but is also the goddess of the forge, craftsmen, art, and poetry. She is a healer and was also venerated by the druids. One rite consisted of hanging a piece of fabric in the moonlight on the night of February 1st so it could absorb Brigid's healing powers. It was the task of the oldest woman in the home to bring in this piece of fabric and show it to the others. Every year the same ritual was performed to strengthen the charms of "Brigid's coat," which was placed on the bed of a woman in labor or during healing ceremonies.

Brigid's connection to nature and fertility was also thought to influence the health of domestic animals.

In mythology, flowers sprouted wherever Brigid walked and she was responsible for the rebirth and awakening of nature, gathering the bees so they would bring humans honey. This dynamic of renewal is also found in the purifying effect of fire. As a symbol of light and return to life after the dark time of winter, fire is at the core of Brigid's cult and virgin priestesses were in charge of maintaining the sacred flame during fertility rituals. Weaving and braiding were also linked to this goddess: reeds and straw were used to form crosses with four branches in the shape of a swastika, a very ancient symbol found in many traditions that was used to protect the home from natural catastrophe. As it did for other moon goddesses, healing water held an important place in her cult and wells dedicated to Brigid became places of pilgrimage.

THE GODDESS OF AWAKENING

Touch your belly and connect yourself to Brigid, the fire woman. Ask her to feed the flame of your femininity. She is the incarnation of rebirth and purification and invites you to respect the shadows, without which light could not emerge. You are these energies: fire and water, heat and cold, clarity and obscurity. She teaches us to respect each one and find life within this mixture.

BIBLIOGRAPHY

Marie-France Arnold, *Sciences et puissance de la Lune,* Irédaniel éditeur, 1991

Véronique Barrau, *Plantes porte-bonheur,* Plume de carotte, 2012

Opakiona Blackwood, Avy Raé, *Almanach des sorcières,* Contre-dires, 2016

Jean Shinoda Bolen, *Goddesses in Every Woman: Powerful Archetypes in Women's Lives,* Harper Collins, 2014

Jacques Brosse, *Mythologie des arbres,* Payot, 1993

Simone Butler, *Moon Power,* Fair Winds Press, 2017

Françoise Dunand, *Isis mère des dieux,* Actes Sud, 2008

Barbara Ehrenreich, Deirdre English, *Sorcières sages-femmes et infirmières,* Cambourakis, 2015

Mircea Eliade, *Le Chamanisme,* Payot, 1968

Paul Ferris, *Les Remèdes de santé d'Hildegarde de Bingen,* Marabout, 2002

Marija Gimbutas, *Le Langage de la Déesse,* Éditions des femmes, 2005

Kalashatra Govinda, *Atlas des chakras,* Macro éditions, 2014

Miranda Gray, *Lune Rouge,* Macro éditions, 2011

Esther Harding, *Les Mystères de la femme,* Petite Bibliothèque Payot, 1953, 1976

Paul Hariot, *Plantes médicinales*

Paul Klincksieck (originally published 1904), 2014

Connie Cokrell Kaplan, *Les Femmes et la pratique spirituelle des rêves,* Véga, 2016

Sandra Kynes, *La Magie des plantes,* Danae, 2017

Sophie Lacoste, *Les plantes qui guérissent,* Leduc.s, 2015

Renée Lebeuf, *La Lune noire interprète du nœud originel,* Dervy, 2005

Pierre Lieutaghi, *Le Livre des bonnes herbes,* Actes Sud, 1996

Julie Loar, *Une déesse par jour,* AdA éditions, 2012

Jean Markale, *La Femme celte,* Payot, 2001

Melanie Marquis, *Lugnasad,* Danae, 2017

Bernard Melguen, Catherine Sauvat, *Lune, la face cachée de la Terre,* La Martinière, 2015

Ann Moura, *Grimoire de magie verte,* Danae, 2018

Vicki Noble, *La Femme Shakti,* Véga, 2012

Marie Pénélope Pérès, Sarah-Maria Leblanc, *Sagesse et pouvoirs du cycle féminin,* Le Souffle d'or, 2014

Susan Pesznecker, *Yule,* Danae, 2017

Michel Pierre, *Les Remèdes de A à Z,* Le Chêne, 2015

Clarissa Pinkola Estés, *Femmes qui courent avec les loups,* Grasset, 1996

Jamie Sams, *Danser le rêve,* Véga, 2017

Jamie Sams, *Les 13 Mères originelles,* Véga, 2011

Camille Sfez, *La Puissance du féminin,* Leduc.s, 2018

Starhawk, *Rêver l'obscur, femmes, magie et politique,* Cambourakis, 2015

GOING FURTHER

○ **AUTHOR WEBSITES**
La Tisanière Tatouée:
https://latisanieretatouee.wordpress.com/ Instagram : @
latisanieretatouee

Vic Oh:

https://vic-oh.com/
Instagram : @ohvicoh

○ **HERBALISM**
SloWood, to order organically farmed dried plants and sacred herbs:
https://slowoodtisane.com/

○ **WOMEN'S CIRCLES**
SloWMoon, where Stéphanie Lafranque offers women's circles and
accompanying activities: https://slowmoonblog.wordpress.com/blog/

Reconnect with your femininity: https://www.renoueravecsonfeminin.fr/

Red tents: https://tentesrouges.fr/

Red tents in Paris: https://tenterougedeparis.fr/

○ **RECONNECTING WITH NATURE**
Druidess: https://druideesse.fr/

ACKNOWLEDGMENTS

Thank you to my lineage, to Mina and Prudence,
my Goddesses of unconditional love.
To Y., my star.
To M.
To my love.
To Victoria, my moon and fire sister.
To Suyapa and Lama, my word goddesses.
To Marie, my Druidess, for her presence in sun and shadow.
To Camille Sfez, who accompanies me on the path of the sacred
feminine.
To Hélène (@tarot-energie), my dear priestess, for her tarot ritual the
first twelve days of the year.
To the witches.
And, of course, to the Moon and Mother Earth.
STÉPHANIE LAFRANQUE

◯

To all the women who gave me my features,
to the women who raised me and inspired me.
Irène, Nila, Cathy, and Éléonore.
To the women I only know from the surreal colors of Mexico.
Infinite gratitude to Stéphanie, my ancestral friend, for giving me an
entire universe to trace, and to Suyapa for her limitless confidence in
my creation.
To Emiliano, who opened me to the spiritual and cosmic worlds.
MCB, MD, JD, thank you for letting me have a world to myself to draw
and reach for the Moon.
To all the magicians who surround me, thank you.
VIC OH